ULTIMATE LIFE SKILLS FOR EPIC TWEENS

Handy tips, Practical activities and illustrations inside.

A FUN TO READ GUIDE ON BUILDING SOCIAL, MENTAL, FINANCIAL, SCHOOL AND HOME SKILLS TO EMPOWER PRETEENS AND GIVE THEM A HEAD START IN LIFE!

VIVIAN FOSTER

SOMETHING FOR YOU!

Get your printable workbook today!

Scan this code to download.

Table of Contents

Introduction

"It takes courage to grow up and become who you really are."

– E.E. Cummings

If you have a friend who can make pancakes, iron their own shirt, or use an ATM machine, you may be very impressed by them. Tweens who have developed numerous skills can often seem more confident and mature, and they are often considered "leaders" in a group. You may wish that you could do a few things like this yourself. Alternatively, you may already be very skillful at some tasks but wish you could master more.

The good news is that you are not alone! Many of the tweens you know (aged around 8 to 12) probably feel the same. Did you know that nearly all parents feel that it is important for their children to know how to cook, but only 33 percent cook with their children weekly?[1] Here are a few more statistics to help you realize that if you haven't mastered as many skills as you would like, you are probably in the majority:

- Around 28 percent of Americans can't cook—and they're adults![2]
- Teens aren't doing much better. Only 45 percent of people aged 18 to 24 and 64 percent of those aged 25 to 34 consider themselves to be "somewhat good" or "good" at cooking—because they didn't learn to cook as children and as teens.[3]
- Around 22 percent of teens lack basic financial skills, despite the fact that children start developing money habits by the age of 7.[4]

It is easy to see why parents and kids may not have enough time together to learn crucial life skills. A survey has shown that members of a family enjoy an average of just 37 minutes

[1] Brown-Riggs, 2017.
[2] Tufts, 2019.
[3] LaMagna, 2016.
[4] Choose FI Foundation, n.d.

together each day.[5] It is logical that this time would be spent doing fun things together (like enjoying a meal), rather than learning skills like how to sew or iron. In the majority of two-parent homes in the US, both parents work full-time and they may have very little extra time to teach kids important skills, hobbies, and abilities.

You may encounter similar issues at your school. Your teacher may have loads of information to get through and, sometimes, the theory side of learning is so tedious that the students may miss out on simple but super-important information that could get them out of a bind. For instance, if a T-shirt you wanted to wear the next day was dirty, would you know how to wash it in the machine? If one parent was super busy working on a report, and you were hungry, could you help another parent or adult with the meal by preparing the side dish? It is funny, you might say, that some of the most vital things in life are the ones we sometimes dedicate the least amount of time to.

Schools simply do not dedicate enough time to subjects like saving, home economics, emergency care, and other essential skills. Parents can also find it hard to teach their children how to make and sustain friendships because they are not in their child's daily life and do not see the problems their tweens may be having.

It is normal that you may feel a little lost. There is so much to learn, and it may seem like every time you want to learn a new skill (for instance, how to tend to a cut or scrape, or how to put the dishwasher on), you have to make your way through numerous websites, which end up wasting your time.

---

[5] Renner, 2018

Consider this book a kind of "one-stop guide" that contains many of these lessons in one handy place. You can keep it by your bedside and pull it out when you want to learn or improve one or more skills, or you can read it through if you'd like to get an overview of all through all of them! In this book, you will learn both personal and practical skills, including:

- *How to make friends*
- *How to keep stress and anxiety at bay*
- *How to feel confident in your daily life*
- *How to set goals*
- *How to become more resilient against life's challenges*
- *How to make smart decisions*
- *How to lead a healthy life*
- *How to cook*
- *How to undertake home chores with ease*
- *How to handle emergencies and stay safe*

It has taken me many years to learn, hone, and teach these skills myself. I am a mom of two teens. My oldest daughter, Claire, is now in college and my son Neil, aged 13, has just emerged from his tween years. The knowledge I am sharing in this book comes from my studies in psychology, extensive research, and my experience as a mom.

As you read through this book, you will probably find that some skills come easier than others. For instance, you may already be a person who finds it easy to start, maintain, and end conversations. On the other hand, you may feel a bit insecure when it comes to knowing how to safely slice a potato or boil pasta. Your friends and family members probably feel the same. They have skills they have acquired throughout their lifetime, and they probably spent more time learning specific things.

However, it is never too late to learn and grow, or to become a master at something you never thought you could do! This happened to me when my children were in primary school. I started making fun cakes at Halloween, and what began as a small hobby soon became a passion. I started making creative fondant cakes in all sorts of fun shapes: skull-shaped cakes for Halloween, chocolate logs for Christmas, and Hello Kitty and Marvel character-shaped cakes for birthdays. Remember that most people are not inherently "good" or "bad" at things. Acing an activity simply involves dedicating time to it, being consistent, and having the resources you need to pursue it. This is why the support of your parents is important if you are to be your best self.

If there is anything in this book you don't understand or need guidance with, show it to a parent or a trusted adult and ask them to clarify what you need or to share their own opinions on specific topics with you.

Parents sometimes complain about social media and the influence that creators can have on children, but there are so many good examples out there. For instance, *Euphoria* star, Sydney Sweeney, is an ace at car mechanics and she has completely renovated an old vehicle. Famous chef Jamie Oliver's 10-year-old son, Buddy, is a skilled cook, and he frequently uploads videos of himself cooking in his family's beautiful garden.

Confidence is also something that can grow over time. Oscar-winning actress Jennifer Lawrence, for instance, had difficulty making friends when she was a tween, and she actually moved schools several times. Meanwhile, Kendall Jenner, who is a beautiful and popular millionaire, was recently laughed at on social media because she didn't know how to cut a cucumber. Of course, this isn't fair at all. Kendall was very young when she started modeling and probably did not have time to hone her cooking skills. The good news for her and anyone in this situation is that it literally is never too late to pick up a skill that you are interested in.

My main goal is to make you feel more confident and eager to try out new skills as you make your way through the chapters in my book. I promise that there will be fun activities to try— including throwing a party for your family or surprising your parents by doing chores like washing clothes. It is important to accept yourself just as you are, but also to continuously aim to be your best self, to expand your knowledge and experience, and to have a great time in life. The more skills you pick up along the way, the more your confidence will grow and the likelier you will be to try out new things.

This book has all you need to enter your teen years with greater confidence. It will provide you with practical skills and easy explanations that will make what some call "chores" seem more like fun activities. I will also share many stories that will help you understand that many of your fears are shared by other people your age. Consider this book a friend; one that won't judge or expect things of you but rather, give you the information you need to shine like the brightest of stars.

CHAPTER ONE
Making Friends

"Wishing to be friends is quick work, but friendship is a slow ripening fruit."

– Aristotle

Having friends is important when you're a tween. Friends can help you:

- Deal better with school problems (such as a tough teacher or a student who bullies or teases others)
- Have fun with people outside of school
- Listen to interesting points of view when you're having a problem
- Have someone to talk to and trust
- Stay out of trouble
- Feel connected
- Have someone to take part in your favorite hobbies with—like dance, sports, or swimming classes

Because you are growing and changing so fast at this age, you may find that your friend groups shift frequently. This is totally normal and to be expected, as you are still discovering so many things about yourself—including your likes and dislikes, the type of friends you enjoy spending the most time with, and the amount of time you need to be with others or enjoy a little "me time."

Challenges for Tweens

Tweens can face specific challenges that can make friendships a source of worry or distress. They include:

Being "iced out" by a friend. Tweens may get very close to one friend in particular, then suddenly find that their BFF prefers to spend time with others and stops responding to their texts or invitations to spend time together. Around 80 percent of adolescents report feeling lonely at some point in time.

The tween brain is still maturing. One part of the brain (the prefrontal cortex, which is in charge of focusing your attention, controlling your impulses, and managing your emotional reactions) continues to mature until you are around 25.[6] This can make it harder for tweens to control their actions or to avoid blurting something out without thinking about it beforehand.

Tweens have a greater need for privacy than in their earlier childhood. At this stage in life, you are trying to find your own sense of self or identity. Wanting your own, private space is an important part of this process.[7]

---

[6] University of Rochester Medical Center, n.d.
[7] Zabell, n.d.

Tweens start facing peer pressure at around the age of 9. Peer pressure is essentially the process by which members of your social group influence each other. Sometimes, it can be a positive thing in your life. For instance, if your friends are all into art and photography, it can inspire you to tap into your artistic side. At other times, however, it can be negative for your physical and mental health and well-being. This can occur if friends try to get you to do things you are not ready for, or things that are only legal for adults—for instance, drinking alcohol.

During your tween and teen years, you may feel stressed by so many conflicting demands—for instance, you may want to do well at school and sports, make and sustain friendships, be a good sibling or child, and similar. Sometimes, it may feel like you are juggling too many oranges at once, and you can feel worried or tense.

Accept Yourself as You Are

As you negotiate your way through school and aim to make friends and be a good student, keep one important thought in mind: Each of us has unique traits and personalities. That means that you may enjoy different activities than others, need more or less "alone time" to re-energize, and/or enjoy having smaller (or larger) friend groups. People generally have more or less of five personality traits:

Openness. People who are very open enjoy meeting new friends and trying out new experiences. Those who are less open may prefer to have smaller friend groups and/or to stick to the activities they already know and have mastered.

Conscientiousness. Someone with a high level of conscientiousness tends to be very organized, hard-working, and goal-oriented. Someone with a lower level of conscientiousness may find it harder to organize their study schedule, or may leave tasks they need to do "until later."

Extraversion. People who are very extraverted are very sociable, warm, and positive. Those who are more introverted, on the other hand, can find parties and other social occasions a little "draining." They may need a little more time alone to feel like "themselves" again.

Agreeableness. People with high levels of agreeableness tend to be very giving, trusting, and straightforward. Those who are not so agreeable may seem a little "grumpy" sometimes.

Neuroticism. People with high levels of neuroticism can frequently be impulsive, vulnerable, and angry. Those with lower levels of this trait can be very well-balanced, as they tend to take time to make decisions and have calmer personalities.

Most people have a mix of these traits. Some have very high or low levels of traits like extraversion or agreeableness. You are still growing and undoubtedly changing from day to day. The important thing to know is that we all have a unique combination of traits that makes us who we are. When you are in the process of making friends, remember that it is okay to just be you.

Accept yourself as you are...

Developing Qualities That Will Help You Make Friends

It isn't difficult to work out the qualities that most people look for in friends. They are probably similar to what you value in your BFF and other friends. Qualities worth developing include:

- **Empathy.** This quality involves putting yourself in someone else's shoes; being sensitive to how they feel and seeing things from their point of view.

  Empathy in Action: Imagine your BFF agrees to sleep over this Friday. However, on Friday morning at school, they tell you that their dad prefers they stay home to work on math problems since your friend failed their last test. If you are empathetic, you will give them a pat on the back and say something like, "Don't worry, I understand. We can get together next weekend."

- **Generosity.** This quality involves sharing time, energy, and, sometimes, material things with others.

  Generosity in Action: A classmate forgets their lunch at home. You offer to share your lunch with them.

- **A Sense of Humor.** Most tweens love being with friends who brighten up their day with a laugh.

  A Sense of Humor in Action: When you have a sense of humor, you make light of a tense situation or conflict by finding something you and your friend can laugh about.

- **Being Present.** Sometimes, someone may be talking to you and your mind may start wandering to other subjects. You may also be tempted to pull out your phone and check your messages while you are talking to them. Being present involves aiming to keep your mind "in the here and now" and giving yourself fully to the people you are spending time with.

  Being Present in Action: Your friend is having a tough time and they want to talk to you about their problems. You put your phone on airplane mode so that your conversation is not interrupted by notifications.

- **Loyalty.** This quality is cherished by friends of all ages. A loyal friend is one who stands by you in good and bad times. They make it clear that you are a big priority for them.

  Loyalty in Action: You and your BFF are having a movie night and pajama party this Saturday night. At school, one of the most popular kids in school invites you to their house on Saturday night. You'd love to go, but they say you can't bring your BFF. You decide to stand by your friend and go ahead with your original plan.

- **Trustworthiness.** Your best friends are often privy to secrets or to private information they do not share with anyone else if it will hurt you. Your good friends are like a "safe." They keep your private life to themselves.

Trustworthiness in Action: You told a BFF not to tell anyone you would be leaving school because you wanted to be the one to let them know about your departure on the last day of school. Your BFF didn't budge. Instead, they kept the information to themselves.

- **Being Supportive.** Good friends are each other's biggest fans. They cheer each other on and console each other when obstacles appear.

Being Supportive in Action: Your best friend loses an important soccer game. You let them know how well they passed the ball and assure them their luck could change in the following game. You spend time with them after the game, having dinner with their family.

How to Start, Maintain, and End a Conversation

Did you know that when you interact with others, only 7 percent is communicated by the spoken word, while 38 percent is communicated through your tone of voice, and 55 percent through your body language?[8] It takes many years of practice to hone your body language skills and to understand the subtle messages that others can send through aspects such as posture and bodily position.

Some tweens may find it difficult to start a conversation, keep it going, and end it politely. The following tips may help:[9]

1. Starting a Conversation

The first step in starting a conversation is figuring out if it is the right time to do so. For instance, if you see a group of schoolmates huddled together with their backs to you, seemingly engaged in a serious or personal conversation,

---

[8] The University of Texas Permian Basin, n.d.

[9] Morin. n.d.

it may not be appropriate to start a conversation with them. However, if you see a couple of classmates sitting during recess, who look up and smile and say "Hi!" when they see you, it might be a great time to join them. Start by saying "Hi, how are you?" or "What are you up to?" If they seem agreeable, continue the conversation, or ask if it is alright to sit down with them.

2. Maintaining a Conversation

In order to make a conversation fun, informative, or valuable, everyone needs to make an effort to maintain it. To do so, show you are interested in what they are saying by nodding once in a while and asking questions like, "How did you feel about that?" or "What did you say to them when they said that?" If you simply nod or say a couple of sentences, the conversation can become a little stale.

Remember that everyone likes to talk about the things they like, so if you know a classmate has a special interest in music, bands, celebrities, influencers, or TikTokers, ask them about it. Feel free to also share your own interests.

3. Ending a Conversation

The key to ending a conversation well is to avoid acting like you are bored and "bailing out." A little trick is to make sure the person knows you enjoyed chatting with them, then share the reason why you need to go. For instance, you might say, "Wow, it's 5 p.m. already. My dad is probably waiting in the parking lot to take me home. It was really fun learning about your *Heartstopper* book collection. Tell me more about it next time." You can also say something simple like, "It was great chatting. I'm off to swim class now but I hope to catch up soon."

Use Friendly Body Language to Attract Friends

We mentioned earlier that body language plays a big role in how well you communicate with others. The body language you use can make you seem friendlier and more interested in what they have to say. To use body language to your best advantage:

- Stand straight and look people in the eyes when they are talking to you, making sure your gaze is friendly.

- Avoid crossing your arms over your chest. This amounts to "closed" body language. Instead, leave your arms by your side and ensure your hands are open. Tightly clenched fists can make a person seem tense. If you are sitting down, try to avoid crossing your legs, as this can also amount to closed body language. Make sure your body is turned toward the person, not away from them.

- If a good friend is very upset, you can touch their shoulder or give them a hug if they ask for one.

- If someone smiles at you, smile back. If they are sad, nod your head and try to mirror their emotion. If they are angry or agitated, look straight into their eyes and use a calm voice and language to reassure them.

Be an Active Listener

One of the most important skills to learn if you wish to make friends is to make people feel like you are really listening to them when they speak. This is called "active listening." It is another skill that takes time and experience. It can be hard to control your impulse to interrupt someone when they are in the middle of a sentence. This can happen once in a while but in general, it is important to make people feel that their feelings and emotions matter. Allowing others the time they need to speak their minds and showing interest in what they are saying are marks of a good friend.

To be an active listener:

- Use open body language, turning toward your friend and maintaining eye contact while someone is speaking.

- Let others fully finish their idea. Concentrate on what they are saying instead of on what you will answer when they finish.

- Show you're focusing on what they are telling you by occasionally saying "I see," "That sounds interesting," or "That must be tough."

- Ask questions if it seems like they would like to go more deeply into a subject they are talking about.

- Once in a while, summarize what they are saying. For instance, you might say, "So you would like to stay over at Mary's on Friday," or "So you feel a little left out when they make plans and don't include you."[10]

BEING POLITE ON THE PHONE

When you call a friend, make sure you use proper etiquette. Identify yourself, ask to speak to your friend, say thank you to the person on the other end of the line, and say goodbye to your friend in a kind way. If, for instance, you call your friend and their parent answers the phone, the following phrases may be useful:

"Good evening, this is John."

"May I please speak to Jamil?"

"Thank you."

"Hi Jamil, this is John. I was calling because I forgot to write down the number of the math exercise we had to do for homework. Could you let me know what it is?"

"That's fab. Thanks, Jamil. See you at school tomorrow."

---

[10] Raising Children, n.d.-a

Where Can You Meet New Friends?

 You can make a friend for life just about anywhere: at school, while engaging in extra-curricular activities, or through other family and friends. Just a few places to make new connections are:[11]

- *Book clubs or kids' gatherings at your local library*
- *Museums and galleries that offer workshops for kids*
- *Kids' events at the local YMCA*
- *Camp*
- *Scuba diving classes (kids as young as 8 can start!)*
- *Gardening class*
- *The Scouts*
- *Swim class*
- *Gymnastics classes*
- *Cooking or baking classes*

To choose an activity for social interaction, go with something that you love or would like to learn more about. For instance, if you are already a muffin-making whiz, then a baking or cake decoration class may be your perfect match!

How to Deal With Conflicts

Conflicts and disagreements exist in all relationships, and they are not always bad. In fact, you can see conflict as a positive thing, since it enables you and your friends to identify things

---

[11] Encourage Play, n.d.

you may need to work on if you want to grow and strengthen your bond. When tensions arise, keep the following tips in mind:

- Don't let things get out of control. Keep your tone calm, use open body language, and if things are too tense, suggest to your friend that you should get back to the conversation later.
- Define the point of conflict. Try to identify the matter you are in disagreement about. You might say, "So you think we should go to Jan's birthday party on Saturday, and I would like to go to the Olivia Rodrigo concert my mom bought us tickets for."
- Think of positive solutions. Try to find a "win-win" situation. For instance, you might visit Jan earlier in the day and give her the present, then go to the concert.
- Choose a solution that everyone agrees on. Friends are equal. Even though you may need to compromise sometimes to make a friend happy, they should do the same for you on other occasions.
- Respect others' opinions, even if you do not agree with them.
- Avoid language like "you always" or "you never" as this makes people feel defensive.

Dealing With Bullying

One in five students says they have been bullied.[12] Bullying can consist of physical aggression, spreading rumors about someone, or excluding them from group activities to be mean. Many kids are cyberbullied, with others sharing content about them or making mean comments online. Avoid places where bullying commonly happens in your school (it might be the lockers or the bathroom), ignore cruel comments, and try to distance yourself from bullies.

If someone follows you and continues saying or doing harmful things, tell them "Stop," or "That's enough," without raising your voice.

If you are being bullied, tell your parents and school about it immediately, so you can nip the problem in the bud. Write down any instance of bullying, including information such as the date and time, what happened, and the place where the incident occurred. This information will be useful for your teachers and parents.

---

[12] PACER, n.d.

Practicing Online Safety

To avoid being cyberbullied, make sure you have your Internet safety strategies down pat. Make sure your password is strong, do not share private or intimate photos of yourself, and be careful of what you write or upload. Remember that information travels at lightning speed on the Internet, and even though you delete something, others may have already shared it. Privatize all your social media accounts so that only authorized people can view your content. Finally, don't meet online friends in real life. People sometimes "catfish" others, pretending to be someone they are not. This can be dangerous and can be avoided by keeping online interactions on the Internet.[13]

TIPS FOR PARENTS

When your children are in the process of making new friends, let them know that they are in charge of their bodies and minds.

Teach them to assert their boundaries by:

- **Letting others know they are not comfortable with certain things.** Give examples. For instance, if they don't like

---

[13] Scholastic, n.d.

being hugged without asking, they can say, "I'd prefer it if you asked me before hugging me." If someone is talking too loud, and it is hurting their ears, they can respectfully ask, "Could you kindly speak a bit softer?"

- **Buy your child a journal and ask them to use it to write down the things they are uncomfortable with.** Their list can include hitting, pushing, being forced to do things they don't want to, and being pressured to do unsafe things. Next to each item on the list, you can work alongside them to identify positive ways they can deal with someone who is disrespecting their boundaries. For instance, if your child writes that they are uncomfortable when somebody takes their snacks without asking, a solution could be to tell the friend, "Please ask next time you want a snack."

Making friends is one of the most magical experiences you will enjoy in your life. It can be a bit hard at first, especially if you are a little shy or you don't enjoy big public occasions. However, being friendly is a skill you can easily learn by following the tips I shared with you. These include using friendly body language, being an active listener, and resolving conflicts with a "win-win" mentality. In the next chapter, we will focus on you, delving into how you can grow your confidence.

CHAPTER TWO
Growing Your Confidence

"When you're different, sometimes you don't see the millions of people who accept you for what you are. All you notice is the person who doesn't."

— Jodi Picoult

There are two skills that all people should strive to improve because they can have such a big influence on your life and happiness. They are self-esteem and self-confidence. When you are confident, it is easier to make friends, try out new things, and feel happier in school. When you have good self-esteem, you don't try to prove how good you are or feel hurt when others put you down because you know your value.

What Is the Difference Between Self-Esteem and Self-Confidence?

Self-esteem and self-confidence are similar in some ways and different in others. Self-esteem is more about how much you value and appreciate yourself. It can change depending on your life experiences. For instance, children who are criticized often can have low self-esteem.

Self-confidence is a belief in yourself and your abilities. For instance, you may feel very confident speaking in public because you know that you can think "on your feet." You may be confident about how you play basketball because you have great aim. Your self-confidence in specific skills grows the more you practice them and the better you become.[14]

---

[14] The University of Queensland, n.d.

Parent and Tween Time:
Take a look at the following statistics with a parent or trusted adult and tell them what you think about them.

Statistics for Parents and Tweens to Read Together

Self-esteem expert, Jack Canfield (the writer of *Chicken Soup for the Soul*) has found that 80 percent of children entering the first grade scored high in self-esteem. By the fifth grade, only 20 percent of the children were scoring positively. And by the time they graduated from high school, that number was down to just 5 percent.

How Can You Improve Your Self-Esteem?

You may have various beliefs about yourself. Sometimes, they are distorted by negative experiences, criticism, and judgment. The following techniques will help you turn these negative beliefs around, so you can see yourself in a more positive light.

ACTIVITY TIME!

From this point onward, I will ask you to keep a journal. You may already have a journal or diary where you write your thoughts, emotions, and experiences. Open a blank page in it and write down a few negative messages you may say to yourself. People can be very hard on themselves without realizing it. They may tell themselves painful things like:

- "I'm so dumb."
- "Other kids just don't like me."
- "Sarah thinks I'm uncool."
- "I'll never learn how to write."
- "I'm ugly. I wish I looked like Sam."
- "My nose/face/hair is ugly."
- "I'm hopeless at public speaking."

Next to these statements, try to think of times that proved that they were wrong. For instance, you might say, "My teacher said I had a very interesting point of view when we were studying poetry the other day," "Ahmed, Grace, and I had a fun time at baseball the other day. They said we should hang out on Saturday and Grace invited us to her house," or "I had trouble writing down a couple of sentences, but now I can write a full paragraph when we're analyzing poetry in class."

Please use these extra pages to write down your thoughts:

Your Negative Comments About Yourself	Positive Comments To Counter The Negative talk About Yourself

Your Negative Comments About Yourself	Positive Comments To Counter The Negative talk About Yourself

Recognizing Your Strengths

Some kids feel that recognizing their strengths is the same as bragging or not being humble. In fact, knowing the areas you excel in (and the areas you may need to work on) is a life skill that will help you throughout your life. Think about the things you like the most about yourself and write them down in your journal.[15] Recognizing your strengths is more about telling yourself positive things than bragging to others. Your strengths may include:

"I like the way I keep trying to learn something even when it's hard."

"I love the way I can draw my family members or pets and somehow, my portraits seem to really capture the expression in their eyes."

"I like the way I can laugh at myself with my BFFs."

"I like the fact that I protect my little brother."

"I'm pretty fast at solving math problems."

"I enjoy helping someone when they're in need."

"I like listening to others when they're down and need a friend to talk to."

Know that one of the most important things in life is to make an effort. Sometimes, you may not achieve the end result you want. However, when you know you have given it your all, you can

---

[15] Gordon, 2022.

give yourself a pat on the back and think about all you learned while pursuing your goal.

Harnessing the Power of Positive Self-Affirmations

In addition to recognizing your strengths, you can also embrace the power of positive self-affirmations in your daily life. Positive self-affirmations are things you say to yourself to give yourself a little "push" every day. Think of yourself as your personal cheerleader. You can make colorful posters with these affirmations or write a few down in your journal and look at them before starting your day.

Just a few statements that can work wonders include:[16]

"I can do anything."
"My uniqueness is wonderful."
"My ideas are creative."
"My thoughts and feelings matter."
"I am grateful for my family and friends."
"I care about others."
"Life is beautiful."
"The people around me are supportive and loving."
"I will make the most of today."

_____
[16] But First Joy, n.d.

Improving Your Self-Confidence

Self-confidence is centered on abilities. You can learn and enhance your skills and abilities by trying out new things, taking on more responsibilities at home and at school, and volunteering for the causes you believe in. For instance, if you love wildlife and you want to protect endangered species, you might sign up for a charity walk to raise funds for animals. If you are into protecting the environment, you can join beach, forest, or city clean-ups. Taking part in activities that improve your community can help you feel like you can take on any new challenge, interact with new people, and share ideas that can help you and your friends achieve your goals.

TIP FOR PARENTS

If you wish to help your child feel more confident about themselves, be a good role model for them. Show them the value of hard work and effort and when things go wrong, emphasize the valuable things you learned along the way.

Avoid getting angry when things don't turn out as you like. Give your kids plenty of unconditional love, so they feel more confident about trying out activities they have never attempted before. Celebrate imperfections; they are what makes all human beings unique!

Confidence-Building Activities

All these activities can help grow your confidence. Talk to your parent(s) and consider:

- Having assigned chores at home.[17] You might be in charge of hanging clothes out to dry or using the clothes dryer, helping your younger sibling tidy up their room, or making sure your dog's water bowl is always full. Chores can seem boring at first, but the more responsibility you take on and the more you successfully complete them on time, the more you can feel like a "boss" who's got it going on!

- Being more active at school. Your school may have a host of optional clubs you can join. For instance, you might decide to start contributing to the school newspaper, join the school council or offer to help out in some other way, and sign up for any after-school activities offered by your teachers. You can also help new students who start at your school, by asking them if they need help, ensuring they aren't isolated, and revealing a few tips and tricks that will make their lives easier.

- Practicing self-kindness. Scientists have found that being as kind to yourself as you are to your loved ones is a powerful way to battle perfectionism.[18] If you find that you are sending yourself negative messages, pause and think of whether you would talk to a friend that way. If it's not okay for them, it shouldn't be okay for you, either.

---

[17] Watts, n.d.
[18] Ferrari et al., 2018.

- Saying "yes" to a new activity. Imagine that you are great at dancing, and you tend to spend most of your free time at dance classes or practicing choreographies at home and making TikToks. You may have a friend who is auditioning for the school musical. You think it might be fun to join them, as you could then spend more time together, but you may fear you won't be accepted because you have told yourself, "I just can't sing."

A HANDY TIP

When there is a new activity, you'd like to try, and you feel a little insecure about it, ask yourself, "What is the very worst thing that could happen?"

Usually, something that can hurt very much in a given moment—like a friend saying "no" when you invite them over—loses importance as time goes by. Ask yourself how much something that is hurting you now will pain you in a year's time, or in five years' time.

Mistakes and disappointments do not define you; they are just part of the experience of life. They can make you stronger and teach you important things about yourself.

Instead of falling prey to insecurities, give it a go! There is usually room for everyone in a school production. Some kids have so-called "lead roles," others form parts of the chorus, and still others can dance. There is a lot of fun to be had backstage as well—in areas like set decoration, fashion, and makeup. Sometimes, you join an activity for one reason but you get so much more out of it than you imagined. For instance, you could make a whole bunch of new friends while working backstage, or find that you can hone your singing by forming part of the chorus.

Growing your confidence...

JOURNALING ACTIVITY

Scenario	What is the worst thing that could happen?	Possible Solution	Would this matter in a year's time?
If I joined the debate club	I could freeze up on the spot and not remember what I had to say.	I could write my main points on small note cards so even if I forgot what I had to say, I could at least say something.	I would probably have a chuckle about it with my friends. If I continued doing my best and stuck with the debating club, I would improve over time and look at my "block" as a small hiccup.
If I joined a ballet class	I could find it hard to follow the choreography.	I could ask the teacher to record the choreography so I could practice at home.	No, because I would either learn the choreographies or get so bored I would try another activity. The important thing is to give it a go and try to learn a few steps. I don't have to dance like Maddie Ziegler.
If I went to summer camp	I could fight with my friends, get bitten by ants, and hate the food.	I could use the conflict resolutions I learned in Chapter One, apply insect repellent, and bring a few non-perishable snacks from home.	Not really, I would have only remembered the best parts of the summer camp and not the negative ones.

Your turn...

JOURNALING ACTIVITY

Scenario	What is the worst thing that could happen?	Possible Solution	Would this matter in a year's time?

JOURNALING ACTIVITY

Scenario	What is the worst thing that could happen?	Possible Solution	Would this matter in a year's time?

"Failure" Is an Opportunity for Growth

I wrote the word failure in quotation marks because I want to stress that failure is the world's best teacher. Make the most of it by:

1. Remembering that you can learn new skills and abilities throughout your lifetime. Just because you failed at something once does not mean you will do so every time.

2. Celebrating failure. Give your sibling a high-five every time one of you "fails."

3. Remembering the acronym for FAIL (First Attempt in Learning). Even if you didn't make it on your second, third, or fourth attempt, the whole fun lies in refusing to let it get you down and trying a new strategy so you have a better outcome next time.

4. Asking yourself, "What did I learn from this experience?" or "What could I try changing next time?"

5. Building your resilience with mindfulness. This involves accepting that you may be sad, frustrated, or even a little angry. You can honor these feelings instead of fighting them, riding through them as you would a high wave in the ocean. Eventually, you can reach a more peaceful part of the water, and watch the wave disappear. Do not push negative emotions away, but don't allow them to take over your peace of mind either. Remember that these emotions are temporary. They do not define who you are.[19]

---

[19] Calm Kids, 2022.

6. Remembering "the learning pit." This is an idea formulated by author and speaker, James Nottingham. It states that when human beings face challenges, they enter a pit of uncertainty and they begin to ask themselves important questions and face hard thoughts like "I've made a mistake," or "I'm stuck on this problem and I don't know what to do." These thoughts are extremely valuable because they show that you are engaging in deeper thinking and learning. As Nottingham asked his readers, "Do you get the sense of 'Eureka!' without having first struggled?"[20]

---

[20] Louick, 2022b.

A TRUE STORY

I remember that when my daughter Claire's friend Yasmin was in middle school she used to get stuck on many math problems. Yasmin would often come over to our house and, when she and Claire had doubts, they would ask for my help. I used to teach them how to solve a problem, then remind Yasmin to review what we had discussed when she got home.

Yasmin didn't enjoy reviewing, so when the next math test came around, she found that she had too much to learn all at once. She pulled out all her notes but found that it was hard to memorize so many concepts all at once.

Yasmin failed the test by very few points, but when she came over after school that day, she vowed to review her notes. She set a goal of achieving at least 70 percent on the next exam. She reviewed the problems I explained every day, and on weekends, she reviewed the whole week's content. The next time they had a test, she achieved an impressive 82 percent! She felt so motivated by her success that she changed her whole way of studying.

She realized that by reviewing her work frequently, she could remove a big weight from her shoulders and face exams confidently. She discovered that tests were actually a great way to show what she already knew.

Don't Compare Yourself to Other

In the Introduction and Chapter One, I explained that at around age 9, tweens can start experiencing peer pressure. It is normal at your age to be influenced by your peers. One thing you should avoid doing is comparing yourself to others because it can damage your self-esteem. Remember that you are unique and that everyone has their strengths, as well as areas that they can work on.

TIPS FOR PARENTS

Try to avoid comparing your child to others or using phrases like, "Gina studies for three hours every day," "Noah reads a book a week," or "Asher won every race he participated participated in." When you compare your child to others, it teaches them to look to others their own value.

It indicates that they should be "rating" themselves as "better" or "worse" than someone else. The problem with comparison is that there is always someone who will be faster, smarter, more graceful, and similar. Your child's goal should not be to be THE best but THEIR best. Happy people evaluate themselves internally, not by comparing themselves to others.

Celebrating Others' Success

Being happy when things go well for others makes you appealing as a friend, and it frees you from the pain of jealousy and other negative emotions that can arise when you base your self-worth on being "better" than others.

I hope that this chapter has helped you understand why it is so important to work on both your self-esteem and self-confidence. You can achieve this by reframing negative beliefs about yourself, trying out new things, celebrating your individuality, and taking on new responsibilities.

Be kind enough to yourself by avoiding comparing yourself to others. Always try to do your best but if you "fail," celebrate everything you learned along the way and see the experience as the best teacher you will ever have. If you are starting to feel more confident, you might just be ready to set new goals. Go to Chapter Three to learn how having and pursuing goals can help strengthen your confidence and resilience!

CHAPTER THREE
Setting Goals

"Your goals are the road maps that guide you and show you what is possible for your life."

– Les Brown

Working toward goals can help you feel like you know where you're going, and you don't need to wait until you are older to start doing so. Just a few goals a tween may have include making the track team, lifting your marks in science, or making a couple more friends when the new school year starts. Studies have shown that people who set goals and schedule their actions are 76 percent more likely to get what they want.[21]

Fun Tip: If you have a goal, write it down! Doing so increases your chances of achieving it by 43 percent!

Why Is Setting Goals Important?

Goals give you something to look forward to. They enable you to feel like you're progressing, and they can help you feel more confident about your ability to work for what you want. Setting goals has a myriad of additional benefits. They include:[22]

- **Self-motivation.** Sometimes, it's just you and your goal, and you only have yourself to rely on to ensure you achieve what you want. If, say, your goal is to improve your 100-yard dash time from 15 to 14 seconds. It's up to you to head to the track daily or as often as you can to practice. Ensuring you have a good sleep and trying to eat healthy foods are additional steps you can take. When you

[21] A.C., 2022.
[22] Prescilla, 2020.

eventually do improve your time, you may feel very proud of yourself, and so you should! Goals you pursue individually or as part of a group can make you feel on top of the world!

- **Improving your decision-making skills.** Choosing a goal to pursue involves making important decisions. In life, you may have many hobbies and interests that vie for your attention. To select one or more goals, you need to weigh the pros and cons of doing so and you will understand your values better as you do so.

- **Boosting focus.** Working toward a goal requires focus or concentration. For instance, if you want to boost your English grade, then at lunchtime, you may decide to have a little quiet time and use it to read a book your teacher recommends or study a bit of grammar. It's easy to get distracted by social media, gaming, and friends (and all these have a place in your life). However, when you have a goal, it becomes easier to avoid distractions when you need to work hard.

- **Having a sense of purpose.** Most happy people feel that they have a purpose or meaning in life. This purpose can be obtained from many things, including good relationships, fun hobbies, sports, entertainment, and other pursuits. Your goal can be full of purpose. For instance, you may decide to find ways to raise funds for a local cancer hospice. You and a friend might decide to knit cute figurines and sell them to raise money for the hospice. As you start knitting more and more dolls and noticing how much people love them, you may enjoy a unique feeling of fulfillment. When your goals have meaning, they enrich you and help you feel you are part of a powerful energy that uplifts you and others.

- **Knowing the value of perseverance.** You may not crack a difficult math problem the first time you try, nor the second. You may put it to the side and get back to it and still be baffled by how to solve it. Eventually, you might log onto Khan Academy or find a brilliant YouTube tutorial that explains the problem and actually gives you handy tricks, so you can solve it quickly and accurately every time! That feeling of discovery is indescribable, and it marks some of the most enjoyable moments in your learning curve. Cherish it, write it down, and never forget what you learned!

- **Learning the value of failure.** I have written about how I feel the word failure doesn't quite capture the wonderful sense of growth, discovery, and fascination that not achieving what you wanted can bring. If I could, I would replace this word with "growth through new discovery" because, in a way, failure is very much like a surprise that can open new doors you never even knew existed. Failure is only true to its name when you don't try to find value in it. Remember to reframe failed goals into new strategies that can help you achieve your goal next time.

How to Set Goals

S. M. A. R. T.

SPECIFIC **MEASURABLE** **ACHIEVABLE** **REALISTIC** **TIME-RELATED**

There is a handy acronym you can use to set your goals. It's called SMART and it stands for:[23]

- **Specific.** Your goal should be very clear so you know exactly when it has been met.

- **Measurable.** Try to answer the question "How much?" or "How many?" so you can have a real measurement of the extent to which your goal is achieved.

- **Achievable.** Set goals you can reasonably achieve with effort, but don't aim for things that will take you so much time you won't be able to sleep, study, or enjoy life.

- **Relevant.** Your goal should be in line with the things you value and your life and the direction in which you're heading.

- **Time-Bound.** Give yourself a deadline so you can stay focused, inspired, and committed!

---

[23] Boogaard, 2021.

Breaking Up Big Goals Into Smaller Ones

You can achieve big goals more easily if you break them up into smaller ones. Consider it a victory every time you achieve a mini-goal. The following example may help you with goal-setting:

Imagine that your goal is to buy a new pair of Jordans. You have a weekly allowance, but you also make a little extra cash by babysitting your younger siblings, helping your parents with dinner every evening, doing yard work, cleaning the interiors of your parents' cars, and cleaning the bathroom. To set your goal:

- Work out how much you need to save.
- Add up the number of hours you will need to work to save this amount.

  For instance, if you receive a $20 weekly allowance and the Jordans cost $135, then you would need to save the full amount for about seven weeks. However, if you could earn an extra $20 a week through odd jobs, you could have your shoe in about three-and-a-half weeks.

- Reward yourself for every mini-goal achieved. For instance, you might decide to keep $5 of every $50 earned to do something fun.

Setting Goals ⋘

GOALS TWEENS MAY ENJOY SETTINGS

 Boosting your Tiktok following by a few hundred followers.

 Improving your swim time.

 Making a desert for your family every weekend.

Earning money to buy your siblings a gift.

 Working out every day.

Eating five servings of fruit and vegetables every day

 Getting at least 10 hours of sleep a day.

Time Management Is Vital if You Want to Achieve Your Goals

Time management can help you prioritize tasks and work out how much time you need to complete each one. Time management involves:

1. **Setting a schedule.** For instance, in the example of improving your track time, you might commit to working out three or four afternoons during the week.

2. **Avoiding distractions.** There are many ways to stop distractions from getting in the way of your progress. For instance, you might put your phone on airplane mode while you're studying, use a timer to complete exercises within a set number of minutes, or study in a place that is far away from temptations like the TV or a stereo. You might also choose to study in the library instead of at a friend's home. Group study can be great, but if you find that you spend most sessions laughing and chatting with your friends, make sure you get enough study time alone.

3. **Using distraction-blocking apps.** You may need to use your computer or have your phone on for security, but wish to avoid notifications while you are working toward your goal. The following are some of the handiest apps:

   - **Freedom.** Use this app to block any websites and apps of your choosing on all of your devices simultaneously. The app also has optional focus sounds, such as the relaxing sounds you might find in nature.

- **Cold Turkey Blocker.** This app allows you to select the sites and apps you want to block, then set up a schedule to block them. The app has one radical function called "Frozen Turkey." It prevents you from logging in to your computer. This might actually come in handy—for instance, if you want to dedicate the afternoon to practicing piano or you want to make sure you have a good night's sleep and avoid the temptation to go online and chat.

- **RescueTime.** This app is pretty creative! It allows you to put all your apps and favorite websites into one of three categories: focus work, other work, and personal activities. You can then block the category you choose.[24]

4. **Prioritizing your time.** Have you ever had to study for an exam and found that you ended up spending loads of time on interesting but irrelevant information, only to lack enough time to study the main topics you focused on in class? When you have a goal, you need to make wise decisions about how to spend your time. When it comes to studying, stick to the topics your teacher paid the most attention to in class. Go over your notes and use any revision lists or materials your teacher gives you. If you already know all the essentials, then you can expand your knowledge with a little extra reading.

5. **Setting a realistic deadline.** Some goals can be achieved in minutes, others take years. When setting your goals, give yourself as much time as you reasonably need.

---

[24] Pot, 2022.

Time Management...

Tips for Working Collaboratively with Peers

 Your next goal may be a team goal. For instance, your history teacher may have placed you into small groups and each of you may have been asked to design and present a talk about one aspect of WWII—for instance, life as a soldier, the role of women and girls, or important battles. Group work is the ultimate test of your ability to manage your time because the success of a project depends on everyone pulling their weight and handing work in on time. To work on a group project, follow the steps below:

1. **Divide tasks among team members.** For instance, if your topic is "Important Battles of WII," each of you can handle one battle.

2. **Set up a schedule.** For instance, on Monday, you should each have all the images and information you need to summarize. By Wednesday, you should summarize your battle in one or two paragraphs. By Friday, one person can put the images and text together on Google Slides or whichever program you use at school.

3. **You should all then check out the final copy to look for mistakes in the text.** Finally, make sure that all images have captions explaining what is taking place in them.

Succeeding at School

If you follow the time management tips above, you should be well on your way to achieving success at school. Of course, achieving good marks also involves hard work and commitment. To ace your next set of exams and shine in academics:

Take time to create an appealing, ergonomic study space. You can either study in your room or, if you have a free space your parents use as an office or a home library, create a dedicated space for studying that is completely separated from your resting area. To help you focus, make sure your study area is

neat and tidy. Clutter can distract you from work and even affect your mood. You should have a comfortable desk and a chair whose height you can adjust, so your feet can lay flat on the floor. You can also have a footrest to boost foot comfort.

To avoid neck and shoulder pain, place your computer screen at least 20 inches from your eyes (about an arm's length distance). If your screen is on the large side, you can position it a bit farther away. Adjust your screen's position so there is no annoying glare in your eyes. Adjust its brightness to a comfortable level. In general, the screen should be as bright as the environment behind it.

Adjust the height of your screen if you have to tilt your chin or bend or tilt any part of your body. Your screen should be placed anywhere between eye level and 30° below your line of sight. This range is determined by the fact that the human eye tends to look straight ahead or slightly downward when at rest. If you are working by a window, place your screen at a 90° angle from nearby windows or use window shades to reduce any glare.

Sit up straight in a "90-90-90" position.[25] This means that your elbows should be bent at a 90° angle, your knees should also have the same angle and your feet should lay flat on the floor. Your ears should be aligned above your shoulders and the latter should be aligned above your hips.

---

[25] Work for Your Beer, n.d.

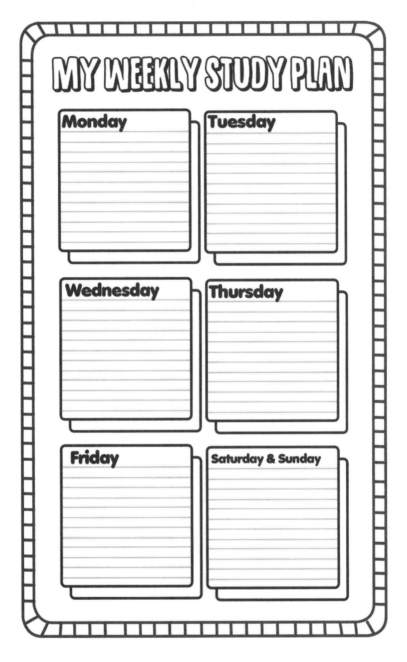

MY WEEKLY STUDY PLAN

Monday

Tuesday

Wednesday

Thursday

Friday

Saturday & Sunday

Create a study plan.

Following a study plan throughout each school trimester will ensure you never need to cram for exams. You may have homework on some days and free time on others. On busy days, you may only be able to handle your homework. On other days, however, take advantage of free time when you get home to review your work. Create a study plan. For instance, on Monday you might review math, on Tuesday you might read and review grammatical rules, on Wednesday you might study science.

Sometimes, simply reading through your notes is enough. However, as you progress through school, some topics may have a substantial amount of notes, and you may find it easier to study for your exams if you summarize your notes.

You can also use a host of tools to make it easier to memorize your work. These include mnemonic devices such as acrostics—using the first letter of every word to remember something, such as "Please Excuse My Dear Aunt Sally" to remember the order of operations in algebra (Parentheses, Exponents, Multiplication and Division, Addition and Subtraction).

Mind maps are also great. They involve the use of colors, images, and words to create posters that can make it easier to learn information.[26] For instance, if you are studying the animal kingdoms, you might have a circle in the center of your page saying "Animal Kingdoms." From this circle, you could have five "branches" that lead to the different kingdoms: animals, plants, fungi, protists, and monerans. You could include cut-out pictures or drawings of these animals and use colored pens to

---

[26] Good Parenting Brighter Children, n.d.

add information about them. Make them funny and unique so you are more likely to remember them!

Using Online Resources

Sometimes, even though your teacher has explained a topic at school, you may be stumped about something. The first step is to be assertive and to ask them to resolve your doubts before they become obstacles to further learning. You can also use online resources to expand on the information taught in class and to explain problems you may be stuck on. If a specific area confuses you, try to not only answer your questions but also delve deeper into the subject. This is one way to turn what you thought was a "weakness" into a strength.

Giving Back

Giving your time, effort, and kindness to those in need can be much more rewarding than receiving lots of presents. It can help you understand your importance: you can make a big difference in this world! In case you were in doubt, these are just a few benefits of giving back:[27]

✎ *Giving your time or sharing your things can help others feel cared for, seen, and heard.*

---

[27] Choc, n.d.

✎ *It helps you feel like you belong—especially if you join a volunteer group.*

✎ *It helps you have a more positive outlook on life and helps you be grateful for the good things you have.*

✎ *Giving is contagious. You could spark a little revolution by encouraging other kids to "pay it forward."*

✎ *Giving is good for your emotional well-being. One study found that patients and their families who volunteered to help other patients experienced greater personal growth and emotional well-being.[28] Other studies have shown that when someone with a health condition offers others with the same condition support, they experience a host of benefits—including greater confidence, self-esteem, and self-awareness.[29]*

✎ *Altruism (giving others your time or doing good) earns you a reputation as a giving person and this makes others more likely to lend you a helping hand. In other words, what goes around comes around!*

[28] Brunier et al., 2002.
[29] Uccelli et al., 2004.

A TRUE STORY

My son, Neil, sometimes gets stuck in math. However, he has a list of favorite sites (including Khan Academy) which usually get him out of his rut. Khan Academy has loads of quick, easy-to-follow videos explaining just about everything you need to know in a wide array of subjects—including math, computing, science, history, art history, and economics.

Khan Academy has an interesting background story, and it has a bit to do with what I wrote before about altruism. This website was founded by Salman Khan, a former hedge fund (investment) analyst who studied at Harvard and MIT. The magic began in August 2004. Salman's cousin, Nadia, was struggling with unit conversion in math. This little gap in her knowledge was stopping her from being placed in the advanced class. Nadia lived in New Orleans and Sal lived far away, in Boston.

He started tutoring her on the phone and then on Yahoo Doodle. She began improving in leaps and bounds and word got around. Sal was eventually tutoring various family members. When he had too many pupils and life became hectic, Sal decided to record his videos and post them on his YouTube channel, so everyone could watch them when they wanted to. He began building up a fan base, and he hasn't stopped since. Today, Khan Academy helps around 135+ million learners worldwide!

Now that you are more confident about your goal-setting techniques, what about accepting a wonderful challenge that will ensure you make it through tough times? The next quality I'd like to teach you is called resilience, and you will need it now and for the rest of your life.

CHAPTER FOUR
Building Resilience

"It's your reaction to adversity, not adversity itself, that determines how your life's story will develop."

– Dieter F. Uchtdorf

n this chapter, I'd like to help you become more resilient. You may wonder what resilience is. It is similar to being strong, but not quite the same. Resilience is the ability to succeed despite the challenges and obstacles you may encounter. When you exercise resilience, it's as though you are a spring that can get stretched without losing shape, because you always bounce back.

Being resilient is important not only for tweens but also for people of all ages. Nobody, not even the happiest people, can completely avoid disappointments, losses, and hard times. However, when you are resilient, you can recover more quickly and still find beauty in life.

Defining Resilience

This section is made for reading with a parent or trusted adult, so you can talk about some of the most important concepts.

Key research has defined resilience as facing an identified risk or challenge yet developing healthily and having a positive outcome in many aspects of your life, over a period of time.

Generally speaking, resilient kids have five main attributes:

1. **They are socially competent.** They build good relationships with adults and schoolmates. They learn and use some of the skills I spoke about in Chapter One.

2. **They have good problem-solving skills.** This enables them to think about a problem from many angles and come up with good solutions.

3. **They have a sense of purpose.** Having purpose means having goals, educational ambitions, and a belief in a bright and happy future.

4. **They have a sense of autonomy or independence.** They don't mind being alone or working out tasks by themselves. They sometimes ask for help but enjoy being independent on other occasions.

5. **They have critical consciousness.** They understand if something is wrong or unfair in the world around them and they desire to make the world a better, fairer place.

One of the best things about resilience is that, like any skill, it can be learned. You may also find that as the years go by and you experience and overcome more challenges, you start to feel more resilient. You may also begin to value the many people, experiences, and things that can help you feel that you can overcome anything.

A HANDY TIP

A Handy Tip: When you're feeling like a situation is overwhelming, remember the words of author Ryder Carroll: "No matter how bleak or menacing a situation may appear, it does not entirely own us. It can't take away our freedom to respond, our power to take action."

Sometimes, a problem can be so big that it can weigh you down and make it seem like you are "frozen" or unable to act. This situation is not who you are, though. It is not permanent, but rather, something you are moving through. When you are forced to face a big loss know that, in time, you will find the strength that comes from adjusting and adapting to the required change.

Real-Life Success Stories

Researchers examined over 100 Romanian children who were adopted by families in the UK when they were under 2. At the time of the adoption, most of them showed delays in development. However, by age 4, many had substantially caught up both physically and mentally.[30]

---

[30] Rutter, 2003.

Another study showed that people who had problems when they were teens were able to change the course of their lives dramatically by making smart choices and taking advantage of the opportunities that were given to them. As adults, they continued their education, learned new skills, and chose healthy life partners.[31]

Yet another study on children with learning disabilities and ADHD found that there are specific factors that contribute to resilience. These are:

1. Seeking to have personal control over one's life.
2. Being willing to look for and accept support.
3. Setting goals.
4. Having a strong will to succeed.
5. Being persistent.

What Strategies Can Help You Build Resilience?

To be more resilient in your day-to-day life, as well as when you meet big obstacles, rely on the following strategies:

Face Your Fears

Take your journal and list a few fears you might have. For instance, you might be afraid of:

✎ *Speaking before your class*

---

[31] Werner & Smith, 2001.

- *Going up and talking to someone you don't know*
- *Exams*
- *Playing a football game against another team*
- *Debating*
- *Performing an individual exercise in PE class*

Work alongside your parent so you can share a few of your fears. Write down a few ideas of how you think you can overcome each of these fears, and ask your parent or someone you trust to brainstorm a few more ideas of how you can do so. Don't tackle all your fears at once. Go one by one, and use your journal to note down the results of the strategies you choose. For instance, if you are shy, you might decide to:

- *Ask someone you get on with at school for their number so you can set up a play date*
- *Go to the next party you are invited to*
- *Join a dance or music class with other people your age.*

After you have tried these activities, write down how they made you think and feel. Remember that resilience is all about persisting, even if a strategy does not work the first time around.

I might be afraid of:	I can overcome this through:

Calm Yourself Down When You Are Stressed

Your feelings can sometimes get the better of you. You may have emotions like anger, fear, or sadness bubbling up inside and they can just "pop," making you feel like your emotions are beyond your control. Know that it is possible to regulate your emotions. Don't feel that you have to push away negative feelings. It is okay to feel emotions like anger. By the same token, it is not okay to insult, hit, or yell at someone else when your emotions seem overwhelming. Emotional regulation is all about recognizing and accepting your emotions while remaining in the driver's seat. If you don't know how to recognize your thoughts and emotions, they can easily get the better of you. Emotional regulation starts by identifying the different emotions and recognizing the signs that you are feeling them.

Never giving up...

A Colorful Wheel of Emotions

Famous psychologist Robert Plutchik created a colorful wheel of emotions to help people identify their feelings. This wheel is made up of three circles. The middle circle contains the eight basic emotions. These are:

- Joy
- Trust
- Fear
- Surprise
- Sadness
- Disgust
- Anger
- Anticipation

The middle circle has a smaller circle inside it and a larger one outside. The inner circle represents the most intense level of the eight basic emotions, and the outer circle represents the emotion in its least intense form. For instance, the most intense version of joy is ecstasy, and the least intense version is serenity. The most intense level of anger is rage, and the least intense level is annoyance.

I suggest that you print an image of the wheel of emotions and keep it inside your school diary or somewhere that is easily accessible at all times. Open your diary to the wheel frequently and try to put your finger somewhere on the wheel to describe what you are feeling at a given moment. For instance, if you learn something super interesting in class, you might describe your emotion as amazement. On the other hand, if someone keeps chatting while you are trying to work, the appropriate emotion might be called distraction.

Knowing what emotion, you are feeling can help you take action if you need to. For instance, if you are angry or feeling rage, it may be time to take a time-out and enjoy a little "me time." Heading to a natural area like your garden and practicing a little belly breathing (a technique I will share with you in Chapter Seven) can help you calm down.

If you are very angry, it can be extremely difficult to solve a problem or resolve a conflict with someone else. Once you know what you are feeling, recognize and respect this emotion, without allowing it to take over your body and mind. Mindfulness is an important technique that teaches you to "ride through" different emotions. I will explain more about this technique in Chapter Seven.

Allow yourself to make mistakes and look at the ways you have grown from them. Mistakes are one of life's greatest teachers because they enable you to adopt healthier strategies to deal with similar challenges in the future.

Be Grateful

By being grateful, even on the worst days, you can see the wonderful things and people that are in your life.

Be Kind to Yourself

Being good to yourself is especially important if you are a perfectionist (someone who pushes themselves harder than others to succeed and who can be self-critical and over-worried about making mistakes). Studies have shown that self-kindness enables people to battle the damaging effects of perfectionism.[32]

Self-kindness can also help switch off your "fight or flight response." This response happens when you perceive that you are under threat. Your body gets ready to either battle the threat or run away from it. The fight or flight response is useful if you are in a dangerous situation, but if you aren't actually facing a threat, it can be bad for your health.

Have you ever heard of "chronic stress?" It happens when people are in fight or flight mode for too long, and it can cause problems for your heart and mind. When you are kind to yourself, your body enters a safe, relaxed spot that is essential for regeneration and healing. It also enables you to be more compassionate to others and to feel more connected to them.[33]

---

[32] Ferrari et al., 2018.
[33] Kirschner et al., 2019.

Maintain Good Friendships and Make New Connections

Friends are invaluable sources of support. They make tough times easier to bear by providing you with someone to talk to and by providing a welcome distraction. Having many friends can help solve a myriad of problems, since a friend may know a solution to an issue you are facing or know someone who can be of help.

Having friends also enables you to feel more resilient because you can help them. When you are there for your friends, you listen to them, and you give them a shoulder to cry on, it is easier to understand your own value in the scheme of things. Composer and singer Ben E. King wrote a song that many friends claim as their and their BFF's hymn. The song, "Stand by Me," says,

"When the night has come

And the land is dark

And the moon

Is the only light we'll see

No, I won't be afraid

No, I won't be afraid

Just as long as you stand

Stand by me."

Play the song if you need a little pick-me-up or if you simply want to celebrate the joy of friendship and support!

Stick to a Daily Routine

Your daily routine might look something like this:

"Wake up, go to school, get home, have an afternoon snack, do my homework for around half an hour, go to basketball/soccer/football/dance/music/art class, go for a walk with my sister and my dog, tidy up my room, take a shower, have dinner, read, do a little meditation, and sleep."

Everyone's routine looks a little different, and yours may involve other activities. However, it is always important to stick to it, as doing so gives you the feeling that you are in control of your tasks, chores, and pastimes— they are not in control of you. When things are cluttered, you are always running late, or you don't complete an important part of your routine, it is easier to feel helpless or lost.

Useful Tip: To keep your room tidy, have a place for everything. Use labeled baskets and drawers to store your things. For extra storage space in a small room, hang pockets on the back of doors, place hooks on walls, and use an over-door hanger. Ask your parents to help you access these handy tools.

Pick Up the Skill of Perspective-Taking

If you have been upset and said something about it to a parent or trusted adult, they may have suggested that you "keep things in perspective." When they say this, they are encouraging you to see the problem from another point of view.[34]

If you love science fiction, then you may have seen the 2004 film *I, Robot*. In the film, the detective chases after a robot that is running with a handbag. The detective assumes that the only reason a robot would be running with a handbag is that it had stolen the bag. However, the robot was actually running because the handbag had an inhaler that was urgently needed by someone with asthma. If you are anything like this detective, you may have wondered why you reacted to a situation in a certain way and wished that you had taken a different perspective before making a conclusion. There is a quote by English miniature painter, James Deacon, which says, "What you see depends not only on what you look at but also on where you look from."

Perspective-Taking Is Important for Many Reasons

1. It fosters the establishment of quality friendships, as it enables you to think of how your actions and words affect others. When you lack perspective, you may behave in a way that annoys others. For instance, you might take their things without asking, share private

---

[34] What To Get My, n.d.

information, or think of your own needs without considering theirs.

2. It reduces stereotypes. Perspective-taking is all about being truly open to knowing and understanding others better.

3. People who understand others' perspectives make great leaders.

4. It can stop you from making a decision on an impulse, only to regret it later.

5. It can give you guidance. For instance, if you and your friend are stumped about an idea, you can approach a parent or teacher and get their perspective. Sometimes, doing so can give you a "Eureka!" moment.

Tips For Perspective-Taking

In order to better understand others' perspectives, try the following:

1. Try to wait before forming a conclusion.

2. Avoid stereotypes about others.

3. Ask others questions so you can understand how they are feeling instead of making assumptions.

4. Remind yourself frequently that people have many perspectives.

An Activity To Try With A Parent

Choose a short story you can read with a parent. You can follow the example of the famous author, Stephen King. He used to read books with his family, with each person reading a page out loud, so the others could enjoy. Try to make sure the book has at least two or three characters. When you are done, look at how each character interpreted a situation or event.

Ask a parent to help you identify why one character had a different perspective from another one. For instance, Mary may have been sad because nobody remembered her birthday, but in fact, everyone was secretly planning her surprise party.[35] John may have thought Sasha didn't like him, but later, he found out that Sasha was shy. Rowena may have been annoyed that Ahmed didn't answer her text, but in fact, he was at a soccer game and when he saw her text, it was too late to answer.

Embrace Change

If you can be sure about one thing in your life, it is that change will present itself many times, often when you least expect it. For instance, your parent may accept a job in another city and you may need to move. Your best friend may leave the school because their parents want them to attend another one. You may be the top scorer in your soccer team, then a new player may join the team and score more goals. You may have one or two good friends in one school year, then suddenly find that you are part of a big group the next. You may be an only child for many years when, one day, your parents announce that you're

---

[35] Speech and Language
Kids, n.d.

about to become a big brother or sister. Being resilient involves celebrating rather than resisting change. It makes sense; why fight something that is bound to happen anyway?

Framing change positively can help when you are facing a development that is difficult. For instance, if you don't do as well on a test as you wanted to, you can understand that this test is just one of many you will take at school and there is always room to improve. A "low grade" is not a permanent assessment of your ability or effort.

PRACTICAL ACTIVITY

Take your journal and make a list of all the things you are grateful for. Here's my list in case you need it for inspiration. I am grateful for:

- My lovely family.
- My friends, especially my childhood BFFs Johnny, Tania, and Nigel.
- My dog, Ella. She is a cute Boston Terrier who is now 13 years old.
- My book collection.
- The free time I have every Friday to have a seaside walk and enjoy a little "me time."

Your list can be as small or large as you like. Remember that this list isn't finite. That is, it can grow as the years go by.

Now that you know the importance of resilience, you are probably ready to start making good decisions and solving problems that come your way. In Chapter Five, I will teach you my seven-step method for doing just that!

Please use this space to write down all the things you are grateful for.

CHAPTER FIVE
The Seven-Step Method for Making Good Decisions

"The problem is not the problem. The problem is your attitude about the problem. Do you understand? "

– Jack Sparrow

M aking decisions is something we all have to do. When you find it hard to make one, or you don't know how to solve a problem, it can be because you lack clarity about the issue. You may not be sure about your priorities or all the available possibilities, or you may be struggling to evaluate your options. The good news is that you can use a practical, seven-step method that is useful for both making decisions and solving problems.

The Seven-Step Method for Making Good Decisions

STEP 1   Identify the Problem or Decision

STEP 2   Name Various Solutions or Decisions

STEP 3   Identify the Pros and Cons of Each Choice

STEP 4   Choose One Option

STEP 5   Test Its Effectiveness

STEP 6   If Your Decision Doesn't Work Out, Try Another Strategy

STEP 7   Use a Journal to Track Your Progress

When you have a problem, you may try to solve it "on the spot" or make the quickest or easiest decision. However, some decisions and problems take a little more time to make or solve.

You don't have to spend hours doing so, but it can help to write information contained in each of the steps in your journal. Journaling is handy for two reasons: it sets the issue out clearly and allows you to look back on your problems in the future, so you can analyze the extent to which you exercised good problem-solving skills.

Step One: Identify the Problem or Decision.
For instance, your cousin Sonia invited you to her quinceañera (15th birthday party) but your school dance is on the same day. Your friend group will be attending the dance and your best friend will be performing his version of a Harry Styles song.

Step Two: Name Various Solutions or Decisions.
 Your answers might look like this:

1. I could go to the quinceañera.

2. I could go to the school dance.

3. I could go to both.

4. I could go to neither.

Step Three: Identify the Pros and Cons of Each Choice.
For instance, the pros of #1 could be:
- I would please my family.

- Quinceañeras are very important parties in our culture, and I would like all my cousins to attend mine when I turn 15.

- The quinceañera will have live entertainment and delicious food.

- There will be a live band and I can dance the night away with my cousins.

The cons could be:

- I would love to be with my best friends at school.

- My BFF has been practicing the song for weeks and is so excited to perform.

- The gym will look great for the dance. I know because I saw some students decorating it.

- All my friends are buying cute outfits for the dance, and I'd like to go shopping with them for something to wear.

Step Four: Choose One Option.
Example: I choose to go to my cousin's quinceañera. I ask my school friend, Serena, to record my BFF during the Harry Styles cover performance. The next day, I call my friend, effusively congratulating them on their performance and saying I can't wait until their next show.

Step Five: Test Its Effectiveness.
Example: I had a great time at the quinceañera with my family and danced with my cousins. The food was great and my dad bought me a great outfit to attend the event. At first, my BFF was disappointed that I wouldn't be attending the dance but understood the quinceañera was an event I was expected to attend. The solution turned out to be effective for me.

Step Six: If Your Decision Doesn't Work Out, Try Another Strategy.
If you decided that your friend's performance was actually more important to you, you might try another solution next time—for instance, ask a parent to take you to both events so you didn't miss out on those precious moments when your friend was performing.

Step Seven: Use a Journal to Track Your Progress.
For major decisions or problems, don't forget to use your journal. The information you write down may be useful now, but it will actually be incredibly useful in the future. When you look back at old journal entries, you may notice certain patterns. For instance, you may notice that you prioritize a certain friend, that you tend to  make the decisions you feel will ruffle the least number of feathers, or that you tend to avoid disappointing a specific person, only to end up letting yourself down. As you identify these patterns, you can work out which ones you wish to correct.

Here is a second scenario and example of how to use the method:

Summer is fast approaching and most of your friends are going to surf camp. However, you've always wanted to learn to sail, and you live in a coastal area with a boating club that offers reasonably priced lessons for kids. Surfing camp sounds like good fun, and everyone from your group is going.

Step One: Identify the Problem or Decision.
You have to decide whether to go surfing with your friends or learn to sail.

Step Two: Name Three or More Possible Solutions or Decisions.

Your answers might be:
1. I could go to the surf camp.
2. I could stay home and learn to sail.
3. I could do neither and read Stephen King's *Dark Tower* books instead.

Step Three: Identify the Pros and Cons of Each Choice.
If I go to the surf camp, the pros are that I would improve at surfing and get to spend all day and night with my group. The cons are that another summer would go by and I still wouldn't know how to sail.

If I stay home and learn to sail, the main pro is that it is the activity I really want to do. The cons are that I would miss out on all the fun at the camp.

Step Four: Choose One Decision.
I choose to stay home and learn to sail.

Step Five: Test Its Effectiveness.
I learned to sail a small boat using just the wind. It was amazing! I met other kids from my area, and we hung out a lot during the summer. I kept in touch with my school friends, and we sent each other Snapchats of what we were up to. When my friends returned, they would frequently speak about how much fun they had at camp. Sometimes, I'd feel a little left out but instead of getting sad about it, I'd ask them to tell me about the anecdotes I had missed. I shared a few of my stories as well about the funny mishaps that occurred while I was sailing. I invited a couple of them to learn sailing with me and they seemed interested.

Step Six: If Your Decision Doesn't Work Out, Try Another Strategy.
Imagine that the sailing lessons were boring, and you didn't like them. Next year, you might decide to go surfing camp instead. In this case, it is clear that the "mistake" was not actually a failure at all. You simply weighed your options and made a decision that didn't turn out as well as you liked. However, you may still have learned vital skills, met one or two cool kids, or decided that you actually don't enjoy sailing.

Step Seven: Use a Journal to Track Your Progress.
By journaling regularly, you will probably find that your decision to try sailing was actually a great one. You may find that in many other instances, taking a risk and choosing the lesser-known option actually worked out well for you. For instance, if another year, everyone is staying home, and you are offered the chance to volunteer for a good cause with your aunt abroad, you may

gain invaluable lessons from this experience. The sailing class example goes to show that sometimes when things don't turn out well, they have nothing to do with you. You often have to deal with plans made by others, and these may simply not gel with you. At other times, well-organized plans fall through because of poor weather or an unexpected event. When journaling, learn to distinguish between the things you have control over and those you don't.

Learning From Mistakes

Mistakes are kind of a secret "gift" that allows you to learn vital things about yourself and others. When you stop being afraid of making mistakes, you can grow as a human being and embrace life to the full. When you make a decision, and you are unhappy with the outcome, remember the following:

1. Resilience is about trying over and over, not giving up, blocking yourself, or turning your back on people and experiences because you are afraid of taking risks or making mistakes.

2. Every mistake takes you a step closer to success.

3. Think about all the effort you put into making a decision or trying to solve a problem. Give yourself a pat on the back for all that hard work!

4. Cope with the results of your efforts. Remember that all human beings make mistakes and that the way you deal with them determines how confident you will be.

A TRUE STORY

In November 2022, the famous singer, actor, and businesswoman Selena Gomez released a documentary called My Mind & Me. In this documentary, she explains that she started working for Disney when she was just a child. As she became more famous across the world, she started to feel more pressure to be perfect as a performer and as a woman. Her mental health suffered, but she kept pushing herself to perform until finally, she broke down.

During her break, she realized that she had done little to satisfy herself as a human being or to protect her health. Today, she speaks about the importance of recognizing and getting help for mental health. She has also founded schools in Africa. If you have started wearing makeup, then you may know that Selena has a successful makeup brand called Rare Beauty.

Recently, she founded the Rare Impact Fund, which supports mental health awareness programs. It has raised $100 million to be used for free mental health services for those in need. Selena's story is one of triumph over adversity. It shows that meaningful things can come out of difficult times. It also shows that it is never too late to make a decision to love yourself, protect your health, and help others who are undergoing similar challenges.

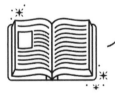

The Importance of Identifying Your Strengths and Weaknesses

Sometimes, making decisions involves prioritizing or choosing one activity over another at school or in your future professional life. Knowing what you are naturally good at is important because it allows you to make better choices.[36] You can focus more on the things you know will give you the desired outcome, say no to things that are unlikely to be fruitful, and plan your choices better.

Knowing your strengths also enables you to reinforce them. For instance, if you find that you love business and dreaming up new ideas, you might join a business club or read up online about how you can start a business as a tween. You can conduct research on the subject, join activities, and talk to people who share your passions and build a better future for yourself.

Finally, when you understand yourself well, you can work better as part of a group. For instance, if you are great at graphic design, but you don't like organizing information, someone else in your group project can organize and assign topics. You can be in charge of putting it all together through your clever design work. This happens all the time in real life. Recently, TESLA co-founder, Elon Musk, told the world how important delegation is. What is delegation, you might ask? It involves assigning tasks to people who are very good at them so that you have time to make other decisions.[37]

---

[36] Make Me Better, 2022.
[37] Egelnick, 2018.

Taking Part in Activities That Sharpen Your Decision-Making Skills

Below are a few games that can help you incorporate decision-making into your everyday routine:[38]

Yarn Maze
This game works best when played with a parent or sibling. Take some yarn and make a maze that someone else has to get through with a tiny Hot Wheels-type car or indeed any small toy (or even a coin). Everyone playing the game can do their best to make a complicated maze with lots of "dead ends" to challenge other players. You can time yourselves to see how much you improve every time you attempt a maze. The game goes to show that things that seem incredibly difficult at first become easier the more you try them out.

Pick-Up Sticks
Use a bunch of pick-up sticks, straws, or twigs to play this game. Grab the bunch of sticks and let them go. Try to remove one stick at a time without moving the other sticks. Every time you move another stick in the pile, you have to start all over. When you play this game frequently, you will work out which sticks are easiest to move and learn techniques (such as lifting one side of a stick to pick it up without moving other sticks) that soon turn you into an ace!

Kitchen Fun
Ask a parent or trusted adult to put out a host of ingredients on the kitchen counter. Once they do, you can choose some of them. Together, you can make a special dish. If you try this

---

[38] Osmo, 2020.

activity out various times, you can work out which ingredient combinations are best for foods like pancakes or omelets.

ACTIVITY TIME!

To cap off this chapter, how about helping out by solving a few problems? Remember to use all the steps in the method.

Please use the space below and write down your "Good deed" of the day.

TIPS FOR PARENTS

If your parents want to help you make wise decisions, they may enjoy reading the following tips, so it's time to pass this book on to them!

As parents, it is normal to want to shield our children from pain and disappointment. However, allowing children to learn from their own experiences is an invaluable lesson that many would say cannot be achieved simply by talking to them.

To hone your child's decision-making skills, try the following strategies:

1. **Allow them to make decisions.** In this chapter, I have shared a seven-step method they can use to weigh various options, make a choice, and analyze the results of this choice. Journaling is important, as your child can learn to recognize the patterns they may follow when making decisions or solving problems.

2. **Give them "real world" experience.** Encourage your children to sign up for activities, embrace the chance to travel, and take part in camps and other experiences that can teach them vital skills. If you "catch" your tween doing something that may be harmful, you might consider reading and educating yourselves together about the subject instead of grounding them. If the idea is to really reach your child so they know why something harmful is to be avoided, then try to open their mind to the truth.

3. **Let your child know that it's okay to try a host of activities and not necessarily excel at them.** It's not necessary to lavish praise on everything a child does, though of course, positive encouragement is always a good thing. A child should know their strengths and weaknesses and be pretty confident when talking about both.

4. **Know your child.** Try to ask the kinds of questions that will get them talking. This way, you can learn more about the decisions your child usually makes (and those they are likely to make). You can then step in with a few helpful strategies or advice when they are about to make an important decision.

5. **Get to know your child's friends.** Open your home to your kids' friends, so you can establish rapport with them as well. Your child's choice of friends will give you information about the type of personalities that gel with your child, and the way they deal with conflicts and disappointments.

6. **Lead by example.** Be honest about your own weaknesses and strengths, and let your child know that it's perfectly fine to make mistakes. When you make one yourself, let your child know what you learned about yourself and how you might change your strategy next time.

Making good decisions is closely linked to the subject of the next chapter: the growth mindset! If you've never heard about it, you will love to know that we are not all born with a set of fixed skills and abilities. Instead, every single one of us can learn, grow, and continuously improve.

CHAPTER SIX
Embracing the Growth Mindset

"Life isn't finding shelter in the storm. It's about learning to dance in the rain."

– Sherrilyn Kenyon

J alissa is a 9-year-old girl who visited a gym to watch her friend, Camille, do gymnastics. She was amazed by what she saw: kids doing fantastic floor routines and working with equipment like the pommel horse and rings.

Jalissa had never done gymnastics before, but she asked her parents if she could join a class at the local sports center. When she started, she couldn't perform a cartwheel and backbends were impossible for her! Her brother Timothy used to tease her and call her "hopeless", but she kept trying and, after a couple of months, her cartwheels were straight and she could almost do a backbend. A couple of weeks after this, she perfected her first backbend.

Jalissa believes that nobody is born knowing how to do flips, somersaults, and cartwheels. She knows it takes lots of hard work to increase your flexibility, balance, and strength.

By committing to gymnastics, going to every class, and practicing in her backyard, she was able to learn some of the things she admired so much in her friend. Camille went on to compete professionally while Jalissa enjoyed gymnastics as a hobby However, Jalissa was ecstatic about the skills she learned and continued to do more incredible moves as time went on.

Jalissa often relies on a growth mindset.

Lisa is an 11-year-old schoolgirl who gets straight As in class. Since she was little, her teachers and parents told her she was very smart. She always got lots of praise from teachers, friends, and other students because she shines in a wide array of subjects and usually receives the top marks in class. One year, a boy called Gerard joined her class. Gerard was a powerhouse at English and seemed to have a talent for writing poems and stories. The English teacher was amazed, and Gerard began getting top marks in the class. Lisa began to feel very worried; the fact that Gerard was doing so well made her feel that her reputation for being the best in English was at risk. To make matters worse, Gerard was also great at drawing and his portraits were ultra-realistic!

Lisa was raised to think that she was born with a set of abilities and skills, and she believed that this was the case for everyone else. When someone came along whom she considered competition, she would become extremely anxious because her whole identity depended on her being number one in class. This led to competitive behavior and late nights studying, so she could outdo the new boy. Lisa was tired and would sometimes feel sleepy in class because she was pushing herself beyond her limits.

Lisa often uses a fixed mindset.

What Is the Growth Mindset?

The growth mindset is a term coined by the researcher Carole Dweck. In her many years of study, Dweck noticed that human beings can have elements of both fixed and growth mindsets. For instance, everyone knows that some activities are very dangerous and should not be practiced. For instance, you should not walk on broken glass without shoes. When facing dangerous experiences, having a fixed mindset can be very useful.

The fixed mindset: People who are often in a fixed mindset may believe that basic qualities like intelligence and talents are fixed. They feel that they must prove their intelligence and spend their time doing so instead of developing them. They believe that talent, rather than effort, brings success.

The growth mindset: People who are often in a growth mindset believe that basic qualities like intelligence and talent can be developed through hard work and commitment. Brains and talent are just the starting point. When you have a growth mindset, you love learning, and you become resilient because you know that you have to keep trying if you want to achieve your goal.[39]

When you are in a fixed mindset, you may:[40]

- *Give up easily.*
- *Avoid hard work.*
- *See criticism as an attack.*
- *Resent your peers.*
- *Feel threatened by others' success.*
- *Feel pressured to prove your intelligence or talent time and time again.*
- *Cry when you get a lower grade than you wanted in an exam.*
- *Hide your struggles from others.*
- *See difficulty as just another sign that you don't have what it takes.*

---

[39] Renaissance, n.d.
[40] Louick, 2022a.

- *Not sign up for an activity or (when you are older) apply for a job because you think it's "out of your league."*
- *Stick to activities you're already good at.*
- *Feel hurt when someone gives you negative feedback.*

When you are in a growth mindset, you may:[41]

- *Engage in challenges to improve.*
- *Persist in the face of obstacles.*
- *Treat criticism as useful feedback.*
- *Feel inspired by (and celebrate) others' success.*
- *See a lower-than-expected grade as a useful reminder that you need to work harder in that subject.*
- *Freely let others know when you are struggling and ask for help from those in the position to give it. For instance, at school, you might tell your teacher if you have difficulty with a concept or exercise.*
- *Feel uplifted by challenges.*
- *Sign up for activities, audition, or apply for a job that looks awesome, even if it seems challenging.*
- *Try activities you have never done before.*
- *See feedback and criticism as invaluable information that can help you grow.*

---

[41] Wong, 2021.

More examples of a fixed vs. a growth mindset:

- The math teacher gives the tweens in her class a difficult problem to solve for homework. She has not taught them how to do it, though she has shared a few basic pointers. Indhira feels angry at the teacher because she "should be teaching them everything they need to know." She gets home, tries to solve the problem, huffs and puffs when she is unable to do so, closes her book, and records a few TikToks. Indhira feels that she was born with a natural ability in math. Therefore, she should not have to make such a big effort to get an A in the subject.

 Farrah usually gets Bs or Cs in math, but there is nothing she loves more than a challenge. She sees the problem the teacher has given them and freaks out a bit. She goes to Google and searches for the relevant topic. She can't find a direct solution to the problem but discovers useful words she can use to narrow her search. She enters Khan Academy and finds an amazing video that explains the problem she is facing. It is hard to understand, and she has to rewind the video at various times, pausing while she makes her calculations. In the end, she applies the method suggested in the video and successfully solves the problem. The next day, she is super excited to share her answer and method with the teacher and class. The teacher is delighted because only three students worked out the answer. She praises Farrah and the latter notices someone eyeing her with a not-so-friendly gaze from the front row. Who do you think it is?

- Sammy and Kenya are two tweens who are introverted. This means that they can find spending time with others in groups a little draining, and they may need a little more time to themselves than their more extraverted classmates (extraverted people love being around others). Both Sammy and Kenya would like to make more friends. Sammy has set himself a goal of doing so. He writes his goal down: "Call up one friend this week and suggest doing something together on the weekend." He calls up Shantara—a girl in his art class who enjoys sculpture just like he does. He suggests that she come with him to a sculpture workshop on the weekend and is delighted when she agrees! Kenya would like to meet more people, but she feels that she is just not the popular type and that she will only make a fool of herself if she calls someone up. She tells herself, "If I don't try, I won't fail."

- Lena and Tiago are learning to dance hip-hop at a dance school. They are preparing for the big end-of-year show in front of parents and friends. Tiago is selected for a solo dance performance. This greatly bothers Lena, who goes home and cries, not understanding why she wasn't chosen. Tiago has been dancing for five years. When he started, he could barely follow a choreography. However, he practiced on weekends and became better and better as the years went on. When he had trouble with specific moves, he let the teacher know, so she could help him or suggest exercises to improve his technique. Last year, when Lena was chosen to perform the solo, he was delighted for her. He knew she was a very talented dancer, and he loved watching her original moves. She inspired him to do better and to learn complex choreographies.

Ways to embrace the Growth Mindset

In order to build a growth mindset, you can:

Tell yourself daily that your brain can get stronger.

Prove to yourself that this is true. Open the dictionary to a random page and learn one word a day or read one short story (or a chapter of a novel) every afternoon. Play a new song every week on the piano until your repertoire becomes huge! There are so many new ways to build your knowledge and strengthen your brain.

Prioritize effort over results.

Goals are important and achieving them is worthy of celebration. However, you should also value hard work. When my daughter was in middle school, before she received her exam results, I would always give her a little present. I would let her know that the gift was for all the hard work she had invested in her studies.

Use the word "yet" to indicate it's only a matter of time before you attain the ability or skill you are interested in.

For example, you might say "I can't run 100 meters in 15 seconds yet," or "I can't play 'Flight of the Bumblebee' on the piano yet," or "I can't do that math problem yet."

When things don't have the desired result, pay attention to the many interesting things and information you encounter.

Think of how this might have made you a more informed, happier, or more interesting person. For instance, while you were practicing to improve your track time, you may have started running with a new friend, and you may have had so much fun that you now look forward to continuing your training together.

Keep the big picture in mind.

Try to think of how much one challenge matters in your life. My daughter Claire's friend didn't get into pre-med at college the first time she tried. However, she did other courses to work up her credits and she was then accepted into pre-med. When she didn't get in the first time, she could have cried, given up, or got into a fixed mentality ("I'm just not smart enough to be a doctor."). Instead, she took on the growth mentality and worked a little harder, and right now, she is exactly where she wants to be.

Challenge yourself if you feel a task is too easy.

For instance, if you've aced the exercise you've been given in class, go a bit further into the topics you are studying or do a little extra reading. Use the extra information you learned along the way, and you will really impress your teacher!

Give yourself permission to fail.

You may fail once, twice, or three times. Remember the words of British leader Winston Churchill: "Never give in. Never give in. Never, never, never, never—in nothing, great or small, large or petty—never give in..."

Celebrities Who Embrace a Growth Mindset

If you love reading about celebrities who overcome challenges, find your inspiration in the following cool people:[42]

Michael Jordan once said, "I would rather be respected than liked." He believed that it was important to pursue your dreams, even if others believed you couldn't. He thought that people who get stuck in the early stages of their dreams do so because they choose security over growth. You have to take reasonable risks if you want to grow.

Apple's Steve Jobs is universally hailed as a genius, and he always surrounded himself with highly competent people. He did not feel threatened by those who were intelligent, and once said, "It doesn't make sense to hire smart people and tell them what to do; we hire smart people, so they can tell us what to do."

---

[42] Jay, 2022.

Thomas Edison

He may be one of the world's most famous inventors, but he made a lot of mistakes to get to where he is. He once said, "I have not failed. I've just found 10, 000 ways that won't work." This statement is the perfect example of embracing challenges and being tenacious.

Colonel Sanders

The famous founder of a popular chicken brand was bankrupt at one point in his life. However, he kept working hard to make his dreams a reality. He once said, "The more I failed, the more I learned."

Kobe Bryant

He was an amazing basketball player who did not let the pressure get him down. He once said, "Everything negative—pressure, challenges—is all an opportunity for me to rise." Even when Kobe had already achieved success, he continued striving to better himself because he wanted to inspire others to be great in whatever they wanted to do in life. Another of his inspiring quotes is, "The moment you give up is the moment you let someone else win."

In the first few chapters of this book, we have worked a lot on building a healthy mindset. In the next chapter, I will go through a few strategies on how to lead a healthy lifestyle. The lifestyle choices you make can have a big impact on your current and future happiness and well-being.

CHAPTER SEVEN
Choosing a Healthy Lifestyle

HEALTHY LIFESTYLE

"Take care of your body. It's the only place you have to live."

– Jim Rohn

T he choices you make now will determine your health and happiness in the present and future. The mind and body are linked, so eating healthily and being physically active can help fight stress, depression, and anxiety.

Important Information for Parents:
The Centers for Disease Control and Prevention (CDC) reports that around 21 percent of 6-to-10-year-olds and 22 percent of 12-to-19-year-olds are obese. Obesity increases the risk of various health conditions, including heart disease, type 2 diabetes, asthma, and more.[43]
Children are also facing challenges in their mental health. Around 9 percent of people aged 3 to 17 have anxiety, and around 4 percent have depression.
Substance abuse and suicide are also important concerns for those aged 12 to 17.

Embracing Mediterranean Foods

When it comes to food, you may have heard of the "Mediterranean diet." In this book, I will be replacing the word "diet" with the word "eating" or "lifestyle." The aim isn't to restrict calories, cut out certain foods, or necessarily try to lose weight. Embracing the Mediterranean way of eating simply involves eating good-quality items from a wide array of food groups.

---

[43] Centers for Disease Control and Prevention, n.d.-b

Handle stress and anxiety...

What Is the Mediterranean Lifestyle?

The Mediterranean lifestyle embraces the food-related habits of people from countries like Greece, Spain, and Italy—those which surround the Mediterranean Sea.[44]
One of the main foundations of Mediterranean eating is plant-based foods like fruits, vegetables, whole grains, legumes, nuts, seeds, herbs, and spices. The main fat used for cooking and dressing salads and other foods is olive oil.

People in the Mediterranean also eat fish, seafood, chicken, and dairy in moderation. Sweets, refined foods, and artificially sugared desserts are only eaten occasionally. They avoid saturated and trans fats.

Tips for Healthy Mediterranean Eating

If you are keen on making the most of the healthy Mediterranean lifestyle, follow these tips:[45]
- Eat plant-based foods every day. These can include fruits, vegetables, beans, nuts, seeds, and whole-grain bread.

- Try to eat as many fruits and vegetables as the CDC recommends. Kids aged 4 to 8 should aim to eat one-and-a-half cups of fruit and the same amount of vegetables every day. Those aged 9 to 13, meanwhile, should aim for one-and-a-half cups of fruit and two cups of vegetables per day.[46]

---

[44] Mayo Clinic, n.d.-a
[45] The Nourished Child, 2021.
[46] Centers for Disease Control and Prevention, n.d.-c

- Choose fresh instead of refined foods. For instance, if you have the option of a cookie or fruit, select the piece of fruit.

- Aim to eat fish more often and to eat less red meat. Some health buffs eat meat only once a week or less.

- Keep your dairy intake to around three servings a day, opting for low-fat milk and cheese instead of full-fat varieties.

What Are Refined Foods?

We mentioned before that Mediterranean eating embraces whole rather than refined foods. Refined foods, which are also called "highly processed foods," are processed or prepared foods and drinks that contain added salt, sugar, or saturated fat. They are linked to various health problems. For instance, people who consume too much salt can develop high blood pressure, while those who eat a lot of added sugar can develop obesity and/or type 2 diabetes.[47]

Examples of Refined Foods
Refined or highly processed foods include:

- *Ready-made salad dressings, sauces, and gravies*
- *Sugary drinks and soda*
- *Corn and other syrups*
- *Jams and marmalades*
- *Ice-cream*
- *Cookies, muffins, and cakes*
- *Processed meats like hot dogs and deli meats*

---

[47] Government of Canada, n.d.

Potato chips and similar snacks
Chocolate
Candy
Fast food like burgers and fries
Frozen foods like pizza and pasta

What Are Saturated and Trans Fats?

Saturated and trans fats are unhealthy fats that are often solid at room temperature. They can increase the likelihood of weight gain and heart disease. The list of foods containing high levels of unhealthy fats includes palm oil, shortening, and lard.[48]

The Link Between Body and Mind

Did you know that what you eat can affect the way you feel? There is a mysterious connection between your brain and the healthful bacteria that live in your gut. Studies show that people who have depression tend to have lower levels of two important bacteria in their gut.[49]

How can you keep your gut healthy, you may ask? The answer is simple: Follow the Mediterranean way of eating! Gut bacteria love fiber; they need it to thrive! Fiber can be found in fruits and vegetables, fortified cereals, beans, and even popcorn! Gut bacteria also love probiotic foods such as yogurt

[48] Medline Plus, n.d.
[49] Recker, 2019.

Jumping Into an Exercise Routine

The CDC recommends that all tweens enjoy an hour of moderate-to-vigorous physical activity every day.

What Is Moderate-to-Vigorous Activity?
Moderate activities are those which get you moving fast or intensely enough that you burn three to six times as much energy as you do when you are inactive. Vigorous activities, meanwhile, burn more than six times as much energy.[50]

Examples of Moderate Activities:

- *Dancing*
- *Gardening*
- *Brisk walking*

Examples of Vigorous Activities:

- *Running*
- *CrossFit*
- *Fast cycling*
- *Fast swimming*
- *Brisk walking up a steep hill*

---

[50] MacIntosh et al., 2021.

Designing Your Workout

Your weekly workout should include different types of exercise, including:

1. **Aerobic exercises.** These exercises make your muscles use oxygen and get your heart pumping. Examples of aerobic exercises are swimming, soccer, dancing, brisk walking, running, doing capoeira, tennis, surfing, cycling, football, and soccer.

2. **Muscle-strengthening exercises.** These include climbing stairs; walking up hills; doing push-ups, sit-ups, and squats; lifting age-appropriate weights as recommended by your PE teacher or trainer; working with resistance bands; cycling; and doing water aerobics. Think of muscle-training exercises as those that make your muscles work a little harder. For instance, water aerobics is considered a resistance exercise because your body has to move against the resistance provided by the water.

3. **Bone-strengthening exercises.** These include running, cycling, flag football, jumping rope, cross-country skiing, as well as sports like soccer, basketball, or tennis, and vigorous dancing. Sports that involve rapid changes in direction can really give your bones a good workout!

How Much of Each Exercise Should You Do?

The CDC recommends spending most of your hour-long workout on aerobic activities. Ensure that you exercise vigorously at least three days a week. Try to include muscle- and bone-strengthening exercises as part of your routine at least three days a week.

Prioritizing Quality Sleep

Kids aged 7 to 12 need 10 to 11 hours of sleep every night. This is a little less than you needed when you were a little kid and a little more than you will need when you are older. When you don't get enough sleep, you can feel tired or sleepy in class, and find it harder to do sports at school. You may also find that it is harder to concentrate and that you feel grumpier than when you have enjoyed a good night's rest.

Quality sleep involves more than just getting a certain number of hours of sleep per night, though. According to the Sleep Foundation, if you are getting good-quality sleep, you:[51]

1. Fall asleep quickly (within about half an hour of getting into bed).

2. Wake up no more than once during the night.

---

[51] Sleep Foundation, 2022.

3. Lie awake for no longer than 20 minutes if you wake up during the night.

4. Feel energized, not tired, during the day.

If you are not getting quality sleep, you may:

1. Take a long time to fall asleep.

2. Wake up numerous times per night.

3. Feel tired and have difficulty concentrating in class or need to drink caffeine to stay awake.

4. Find that your eyes are swollen or that they have developed dark circles.

5. Feel more stressed out than usual.

In order to enjoy good sleep quantity and quality, aim to:

- *Embrace a regular sleep routine. For instance, you might have a shower, do a little reading, then shut off the lights at a specific time.*

- *Avoid caffeinated drinks in the afternoon or evening.*

- *Avoid using screens in the evening as the light they emit makes you more alert.*

- *Try exercises like mindfulness meditation or progressive muscle relaxation if you are stressed.*

- *Try to enjoy at least 15 minutes in the morning sunlight. This will wake you up and make you more alert during the day.*

TIPS FOR PARENTS

Your child's bedroom design can have a big impact on how well they sleep. The Sleep Foundation recommends that rooms be dark, quiet, and cool—since these conditions can enhance sleepiness.

The thermostat should be set to the low-or-mid 60 degrees Fahrenheit (16°C). Blackout curtains, meanwhile, will ensure that your child's bedroom is dark. A white noise machine can help relax their senses if necessary.

Maintaining Good Hygiene

Following a good hygiene routine is very important, both for your physical and mental health. If you don't shower or protect your skin, for instance, you can develop painful or itchy

conditions such as infections and dandruff. Being hygienic is also about protecting your mental health since when you look and smell good, it is easier to feel on top of the world. Aim to follow this hygiene routine:

- **Shower every day or every other day.** Use a sponge and body gel, so you can reach all areas of your body. Don't forget to scrub your toes, the area behind your ears, your armpits, and your back. Depending on how dry or oily your hair is, wash your hair as required and use a conditioner, so your hair is easy to comb out afterward. Use a hairdryer and products like mousse and spray if you wish to create a cool hairstyle.

- **Use a deodorant or antiperspirant right after washing your armpits.** If your armpits get smelly after exercise, don't just reapply deodorant. Wash your armpits again, apply deodorant, and wear a new shirt, as the old one will retain bad smells until it is washed.

- **Trim your nails regularly.** Long nails can crack or get caught in things, and dirt can easily get trapped beneath them and cause infections.
- **Change your underwear and socks daily.** These can easily get smelly.

Natural Stress Busters

Anxiety affects around 10 percent of children aged 3 to 17 in the US.[52] Stress is a trigger for anxiety, depression, and other mental conditions. Even if you don't have anxiety, you know that stress can be very unpleasant. It can make it hard for you to enjoy a moment, concentrate in class, or maintain the good mood you need to sustain happy relationships.

The good news is that there are so many scientifically proven ways to nip stress in the bud. Try out some of the following.

---

[52] Centers for Disease Control and Prevention, n.d.-a

1. **Mindfulness meditation.** This activity focuses on being in the present by bringing your attention to your breath. When you do so, you can observe the thoughts, emotions, and sensations you are experiencing, and become more connected to your body and mind.[53]

   There are many books, YouTube videos, and apps (including Calm and Headspace) that provide wonderful mindfulness meditation sessions for kids. Meditation can include:

   - **Mantra meditation.** This type of meditation involves repeating a word or phrase in your mind or saying it out loud.

   - **Guided meditation.** In a guided meditation, you listen to a person or audio recording that can have a purpose like calming your mind or helping you sleep.

2. **Yoga.** This activity is very popular the world over. In addition to battling stress, it can also help improve your flexibility and strength. Yoga involves performing several postures while also working on your breathing. Some teachers incorporate meditation into their yoga sessions.

3. **Controlled breathing.** By using the right techniques, you can lower your heart rate and curb a panic attack. There are many powerful breathing techniques that you can use to keep stress at bay. They include:

   - **Belly breathing.** To practice belly breathing, lie on your back or sit down comfortably. Take a deep breath

---

[53] Sileo, 2018.

127

through your nose and feel how your lower belly fills up with air. Think of pushing your belly button outward while you take in air. Take several seconds to exhale, feeling your tummy return to its normal position. To practice this exercise while you are on your way to school or when you have a free moment, download the app Breathe.[54]

- **Alternate nose breathing.** Many kids find this exercise quite fun because it involves using your fingers and concentrating. This in itself can help you keep your mind in the present moment instead of allowing your worries to take over your peace of mind. To perform this type of breathing, sit in a comfortable spot. Inhale and exhale completely, then use your right thumb or pointer finger to close your right nostril. Inhale through the left nostril then close your left nostril with your finger. Open your right nostril and exhale through it. Inhale through your right nostril then close it, exhaling through the left. Repeat this cycle for around five minutes.

4. **Progressive muscle relaxation.**[55]
   Lie down on your back and take a breath. Tense up the muscles in your body for a few seconds and inhale. As you exhale, relax your muscles. Start this process with your toes, working your way up your feet, calves, thighs, bottom, abdomen, hands, arms, shoulders, and so on, until you are tensing and relaxing your neck, nose, eyes, and eyebrows. Feel how relaxing it is to let go of tension in your entire body.

---

[54] Harvard Health Publishing, 2016.
[55] Raising Children, n.d.-b

5. **Spending time in nature.** I have spoken about how healing nature can be. One study by Cornell University researchers showed that people who spent just 10 minutes in a green area were able to lower their stress levels significantly.[56] You can obtain just as much benefit by sitting in your garden under your favorite tree, as by visiting a park or walking along a beach or lake. If you prefer to be active and you live in a coastal or lakeside area, activities like scuba diving, snorkeling, sandcastle building, water-skiing, and kite surfing can all do wonders for your body and mind.

---

[56] Meredith et al., 2020.

Vivian Foster

ACTIVITY TIME!

REPEATING A MANTRA:

Find a positive mantra or saying that you like. The following may serve as inspiration when you are choosing your mantra:

"I am friendly."
"I am brave."
"I enjoy learning."
"I am unique."
"Today will be a beautiful day and I will do my best to make it so."
"May I be calm, and may you be gentle and kind."
"I will smile and be relaxed as much as I can."
"I am happy and funny. May I always be like this."

Once you have chosen your mantra, sit down comfortably and close your eyes. Focus on the way you inhale or exhale. Repeat your mantra out loud or silently to yourself. See how the words feel on your lips and the effect that they have on your entire body.

Social Media: How Much Is Too Much?

It is amazing to think that something as fun as chatting online and sharing and viewing photos on social media can affect your mental health. As with all good things in life, the key to making the most of social media is enjoying it in moderation.

A 2019 study of over 6,500 12-to-15-year-olds in the US found that those who spent over three hours a day on social media might have a higher risk of mental health problems. Another study on over 12,000 13-to-16-year-olds showed that using social media more than three times a day predicts poor mental health and well-being. There is also a link between high levels of social media use and anxiety and depression.[57]

By no means is social media inherently "bad." In fact, it has many benefits. It allows you to create cool online identities and avatars, offers a means through which to socialize out of school with other kids your age, and provides support when you need it. To make the most of social media, talk to your parents and aim to:

1. Decide together on a reasonable time for social media use.

---

[57] Mayo Clinic, n.d.-b

2. Be kind and respectful. Behaviors such as bullying, insulting, and sharing others' personal information are a no-no. Remember that once you post something, even if you delete it later, someone may already have captured a screenshot of it and decided to share it. Information travels at lightning speed on the Internet.

3. Know that social media sometimes isn't realistic. In fact, it is full of filtered and altered images and (sometimes) false information.

TIP TIME!

A Handy Tip

Try to ensure that you have a good balance between school and your social and personal life, and participate in activities outside of school. A 2020 study by scientists at the University of British Columbia has shown that kids who participated in extracurricular activities like sports and art (and less time in front of screens) have better mental health.59 These activities help people feel more satisfied with their lives and more optimistic.

By contrast, longer screen time is linked to higher levels of anxiety and depression. The study also showed that longer screen time impacts girls' mental health more severely than it does boys. Among both boys and girls, mental health was at its best when kids took part in out-of-school activities and spent less than two hours using screens.

In the first few chapters, you've learned a lot about yourself. By now you have a host of tips on how to make friends, lead a healthy lifestyle, and keep stress at bay. It's time to turn to practical skills that can boost your confidence and independence. Chores can seem like a pain to learn at first, but once you master them, you will probably find that there are some you love (my favorite is ironing!) and some you enjoy less (I can't stand dusting). One thing that's sure is that if you practice the skills I shared with you, you will feel like you can make it on your own two feet—and that is a great feeling!

CHAPTER EIGHT
Cooking and Cleaning Essentials

COOKING ESSENTIALS

CLEANING ESSENTIALS

"No one is born a great cook. One learns by doing."

– Julia Child

I f you don't know how to cook and clean, know that you are not alone. Even in college, around seven out of 10 young adults say they are less prepared to clean on their own, even though 92 percent of them feel their best physically and mentally when their room is clean and tidy.[58] Below you will find a few tips on how to perform a wide range of tasks, from how to make your bed to how to keep your room clean.

Making a Bed

When you make a bed for the first time, it can seem very difficult. How do you get the sheets tight and symmetrical, so you feel well tucked in? Like most of the tasks mentioned in this chapter, it takes practice, but once you get the knack for it, your bed will always look perfect. Let's get right to it!

1. Get your sheets ready. You will need a fitted sheet (these sheets curl inward at the corner so they can "hug" your bed) and a top sheet, plus a thicker blanket if it is winter or if you live in a cool area. Don't forget your pillowcases!

2. Try to ensure that there is space on both sides of your bed. If one side is stuck against the wall, ask help from a parent to pull it out so you can work freely on both sides.

3. Place the fitted sheet on the bed, making sure the corners of the bed are completely covered by the sheet.

---

[58] Collins, 2022.

4. Next, place the top sheet on the bed, making sure the decorative side is on the top end, where your head goes. Pull it all the way to the top of the mattress and make sure that the sheet is hanging evenly on both sides of the bed.

5. Line up your blanket with the top sheet, leaving a few inches between the highest part of the blanket and the end of the sheet. Fold the sheet over the blanket tightly.

6. Now it's time to tuck in the sheets. Take one of the corners and fold it toward one side of the bed, then tuck in the overhang tightly and proceed to tuck one side in, then do the same with the other side.

7. If you have a thicker blanket or duvet, place it on the bed and fold it back with a thick fold, without tucking it in. Add cushions and an extra soft throw blanket across the bottom of your bed.

8. Place new pillowcases on your pillows and fluff them up, arranging them alongside cushions if you wish to make your bed extra inviting.

9. Change your sheets, blankets, and pillowcases once a week, so they always smell nice and fresh!

Keeping Your Room Tidy

It's easy to feel on top of things and focus on your studies when you are in a room that is clean, tidy, and organized. By keeping your room in tip-top condition always, you will never need a piece of equipment or study tool that you can't find. To ensure you have a neat bedroom, keep the following tips in mind:

1. Sit with your parent and work out all the things you need to store in your room. **Tip for parents:** When discovering all the things your child has to keep tidy (including toys, books, study material, and gadgets), you may find that they need an extra piece of storage furniture, clear boxes to keep items in, hangers to fit more clothes in their wardrobe, and similar.

2. Use labels to remind yourself where things go.

3. Regularly get rid of junk and things you no longer use. Before throwing the items away, you may want to talk to your parent about holding a garage sale, giving items away, or donating books to the local library. You might also want to give clothing and other items that are still in good condition to charity organizations.

4. Have a shelf by your desk. Have different storage spaces where you can keep items like pens, scissors, coloring pens, staplers, and of course, your journal!

Keeping Your Room Clean

Even if your parents regularly vacuum or sweep and mop your room, you can help out by dusting the items on your shelf, using a surface cleaner to wipe down your desk, and using a keyboard cleaner to keep germs at bay. Everyday items can get covered by germs very quickly. ABC News reports, for instance, that some of the germiest items are purses and wallets, remote controls, laundry machines, cutting boards in the kitchen, and your phone![59] You can also ask your parents to help you learn to use a standing vacuum cleaner, which is light and very efficient at removing dust from your floor.

Using a Dishwasher

Using a dishwasher nightly can save you over 100 gallons of water than if you wash dishes by hand for 10 minutes.[60] To learn how to use a dishwasher, enlist the help of a parent to make sure you use the machine correctly.

---

[59] Brownstein & Chitale, 2008.
[60] Chalmers, 2022.

TIPS FOR PARENTS

1. Start off with an empty dishwasher and show kids where items go. Teach them to place plates in the designated racks and to place cutlery in the space provided for them.

Show them how to place glasses and cups on the "spikes" provided for this purpose.

2. Teach your child how to start up the machine. Explain that every machine has its own instructions. Usually, the machine will prompt you to place your soap in the designated slot, choose a cycle, then press START.

3. Once the machine indicates the load is washed, show kid how to stack similar items, so they can be stored in the cupboard in an organized way.

4. Start off with an empty dishwasher and show kids where items go. Teach them to place plates in the designated racks and to place cutlery in the space provided for them. Show them how to place glasses and cups on the "spikes" provided for this purpose.

5. Teach your child how to start up the machine. Explain that every machine has its own instructions. Usually, the machine will prompt you to place your soap in the designated slot, choose a cycle, then press START.

6. Once the machine indicates the load is washed, show kids how to stack similar items, so they can be stored in the cupboard in an organized way.

Using a Washing Machine

The sooner you learn to wash your own clothes, the better! Sometimes, your parents may be busy and/or at work, and you can take advantage of a quiet moment to pop some clothes in the machine. In order to ensure you use the washing machine correctly, it is a good idea to wash your first load of clothes with your parents.

TIPS FOR PARENTS

To help your children ace clothes-washing chores, follow these tips:

1. Take several items of clothing and show children the symbols that indicate aspects such as the temperature at which clothes should be washed, whether they should be machine- or hand-washed, and similar. For instance, kids should know when items should be washed in cold water and when they need to be hand-washed. These labels will also indicate whether or not clothing can be ironed.

2. White and colored items should be separated to avoid staining.

3. Washing machines have clear symbols that indicate the type of cycles you can choose. There are symbols and words like "delicate," "power wash," and "dark wash." This makes it easy to match the cycle with the type of clothing you wish to clean. Show your child how to pick the appropriate cycle and press START after they have added the appropriate amount of detergent and fabric softener.

4. When the cycle is over, place the clothes in a basket so they can be ironed, folded, or placed on hangers.

Ironing Clothes

Ironing can seem scary if you've never tried it before because this piece of household equipment gets searingly hot. Once again, ironing for the first time is best done with a parent. Most parents agree that with supervision and training, kids eight and older can be taught to safely use an iron.[61]

Below are a few tips parents can share with their tweens:

1. Separate clothes by fabric. Some items are delicate and others are sturdier. Let kids know the importance of ironing delicate items first, as the iron gets progressively hotter the longer it is on, and delicate fabrics can get destroyed if the iron is too hot.

2. Show your child how to adjust the iron in accordance with the instructions contained in their clothes' labels. A symbol of an iron with one dot means the iron should be kept cool. Two dots means warm, three dots means hot, and a cross over an iron means the item should not be ironed.

3. Show your child how to use a spray bottle (or internal misting function in your iron) to wet shirts, so they are easier to iron.

4. Show children the order for ironing a shirt. For instance, for a typical shirt with a collar, you would start with the collar, then proceed to the cuffs, the yoke (the top of the back and shoulder section), the back, the front, and finally, the sleeves.

5. The shirt should be well-placed on the hanger, so it does not lose its beautiful smoothness.

---

[61] Zom, 2020.

Learning to read laundry symbols is essential because it allows you to take better care of your clothes and extend their lifespan. Laundry symbols provide information on adequately washing, drying, and ironing your clothes and other essential care instructions. It is a valuable skill that can help you take better care of your clothes, extend their lifespan, and save you time and money.

Helping Your Parents Recycle and Upcycle

You can do so much to help halt global warming. One of the most important ways to stop trash from filing landfills to the brim is to take part in home recycling and upcycling efforts.

TIPS FOR PARENTS

1. Before throwing something away, ask your child to consider if they might be able to use it for something else. For instance, if a shirt has been torn, can the save the buttons, or use the fabric as a cleaning cloth? Can the use items like mason jars, egg cartons, toilet paper rolls, raw pasta, or raw rice grains, for future projects? If you and your kids love fashion, consider making an upcycled jacket. Take an old jacket and bling it up with brooches, bows, buttons, and dreamcatchers.

2. Have different trash cans (or a compartmentalized trash can) for recycling purposes. Teach your child how to place items in the right bin.

3. Take your children with you to a recycling center and give them a bonus with the cash you get back from returning bottles.

4. Organize a "swap party" so that kids in your neighborhood can swap or sell each other unwanted items.

It's Time to Get Cooking!

Cooking is one of the funnest pastimes you could ever take up. There is an added bonus: Food makes people happy. Just think of how you feel on Saturday mornings when your mom, dad, or older sibling announces that warm pancakes with maple syrup and bacon are waiting for you on the table!

It's a good idea to learn how to cook with a parent who is supervising or cooking alongside you. Weekends are ideal because your parents are probably relaxed and may take extra time to cook some of your favorite dishes. Before you get started, remember the following:

Stay Safe in the Kitchen

The kitchen is a place to be creative and prepare a host of lip-smacking dishes. However, safety is important because when you are in the kitchen, you are surrounded by electrical and sharp equipment. To stay safe during your cooking adventures, remember to:

- Always ask an adult's permission before cooking, so they can supervise if they feel it's necessary.
- Wash your hands with soap and water before handling food.
- Clean up frequently. Don't let a load of pots and pans build up on your countertop or you may feel overwhelmed when you have to tackle the mess. Use a surface cleaner to ensure your countertop is clean.
- Use a big chopping board so that your ingredients do not fall on your kitchen surfaces.

- Store ingredients in the right place in the fridge. Most fridges have images on them, so you can see where fruit, vegetable, and meat should go. Some foods should not be stored in the same compartment as they can affect quality and food safety.

- Check that all appliances are turned off when you leave.

Important Tip for Parents:

Before encouraging tweens to cook, have a talk with them about fire safety. Let them know that pan handles should be kept away from flames and turned away from where they may get bumped into or knocked. Let your child know that they should call 911 if a fire starts. Share important tips such as:

- Never place metal or aluminum in microwaves (as this could cause a fire to start).

- Never put plastic into the oven.

- Never add water to a pan with hot oil (because a mist of hot oil and boiling water will scatter in all directions, and you could get burned).[62]

Essential Tools for Cooking

Ask your parents if you can have your own storage space for your special, child-friendly equipment. Talk to your parent about helping you access vital pieces of child-friendly kitchen equipment. These include:

- Child-friendly knives. These aren't as sharp as adult knives. Some of them have a serrated edge.

[62] Spruce, 2016.

- Small knives with a sharper edge (these are usually deemed suitable for children aged 6 to 10). The fact that they are smaller means they are easier to grip.

- Smaller bowls, lighter mortar and pestles, and smaller whisks.

- An apron.

- A chef's hat if you love taking pictures of yourself for social media.

Knife Tips

There are various types of knives. Some are larger and some are smaller and each has its specific purpose. Popular knife categories include:

- **Chef Knives:** These are large knives that are typically 8 to 10 inches long. They are known as "the workhorse of the kitchen" because they are used for many purposes—including chopping, dicing, and slicing.

- **Paring Knives:** These are small, fine, and sharp. They are used to peel or cut fruit and vegetables into smaller pieces.

- **Serrated Knives:** These knives have a serrated edge, which makes it easier to cut bread, cheese, and soft fruits and vegetables.

Knife Skills

There are many skills that make using knives safer. Remember to cook with a parent, especially when using sharp utensils like knives.

TIPS FOR PARENTS

1.To teach your kids to use a knife safely and confidently:

2. Buy them a knife with a guard. These guards are located between the blade and the knife handle.

3. Teach them to cut round vegetables like zucchini laterally to make a flat surface. This way, the vegetables won't roll around while they are being chopped or sliced.

4. Teach your child to avoid placing their pointer finger on top of the blade, so they learn how to grip the knife well.

5. Teach them to round out the hand that is holding the food so that it resembles a claw. Their thumb should be tucked into this claw. Mastering this way of holding ingredients is challenging at first, but it is a surefire way to stop kids' fingers from getting in the way when they are cutting food.

6. Use a solid cutting board and place a damp cloth underneath it to make it more stable.

7. Teach children to avoid reaching for something within the space of someone who is cutting a food item, and make sure everyone who is cooking has enough space to move around and work safely.

Safety in the kitchen...

How Do You Read a Recipe?

If you look at popular recipe sites online, you will find that recipes are made up of:

- General information on how long the recipe takes to prepare and how many people it feeds.

- An ingredients list that indicates all the items you need to make a dish.

- Instructions that let you know how you should prepare different ingredients and put them all together.

- Cooking temperatures and times that are crucial to follow if you want your dish to come out "just right."

Measuring Food

When it comes to cooking and baking, you may find that most recipes measure ingredients by cups, tablespoons, teaspoons, and similar. Liquids, meanwhile, are sometimes measured in cups but also in pints, quarts, and gallons. In countries like the UK, where the metric system is used, liquids are usually measured in milliliters or in liters.

These terms are actually very specific. For instance, when a recipe calls for "one cup of flour," it does not mean any old cup or mug. Cups and spoons for cooking and baking need to be bought. Cake recipes, in particular, require you to follow measurements exactly so investing in these tools is vital. The good news is that you can get your hands on these measurement tools for just a few dollars or pounds.

Typical cup measurements include one cup, one-half cup, one-quarter cup, and similar.

Typical spoon measurements include one tablespoon, one-half tablespoon, one-quarter tablespoon, one teaspoon, one-half teaspoon, one-quarter teaspoon, and similar. Tablespoons are larger than teaspoons.

Tip for Measuring Dry Ingredients

When you have to measure dry ingredients like flour, sugar, or powdered sugar, spoon your ingredients into the measuring cup, then level off any excess with the flat side of a knife. The cup should be completely flat, to make sure your cakes, cupcakes, and cookies do not change in quality every time you prepare the recipe. You can also use this technique when measuring dry ingredients with tablespoons and teaspoons.

Common Cooking Terms

Recipes often tell you to "slice," "dice," or "chop" food. While all these techniques involve turning a larger food item into smaller or finer pieces, each is specific. Just a few terms you should be familiar with are:[63]

---

[63] Raddish Kids, n.d.

COMMON COOKING TERMS

Bake: To cook savory or sweet foods in the oven.

Beat: To mix rapidly with a whisk, electric mixer, or fork to bring air into a mixture and make it light and smooth.

Boil: To heat liquid up until it starts bubbling up and, sometimes, to cook something in this liquid.

Bread: To coat an ingredient with breadcrumbs.

Chop: To cut into small pieces.

Core: To remove seeds or the tough center from fruits or vegetables.

Deseed: To remove the seeds from produce.

Dice: To cut into small squares or cubes.

Fry: To cook food in hot oil or butter.

Garnish: To decorate a dish with an edible ingredient.

Grate: To shred food by putting it through a grater.

Grease: To coat a pan in butter or another fat so that food does not stick to it when you bake it.

Drain: To use a strainer to remove liquid from an item. For instance, you might drain the water away from pasta after it is cooked.

Marinate: To place food in a sauce for a while (between half an hour to overnight) so it soaks up more flavor or becomes more tender.

Pan-fry: To cook food in a skillet with a little fat.

Peel: To remove the peel of fruits or vegetables.

Sauté: To cook food in a small amount of fat over high heat.

Season: To add salt, pepper, and other seasonings to ingredients.

Setting a Table

If you have cooked something nice for your family and you also want to set the table correctly, follow these steps:

1. Place the big plate (the dinner plate) in the middle. Place a small bread plate to the left of the dinner plate and a drinking glass to the right of the dinner plate.

2. Place a napkin in the middle or to the right of the dinner plate.

3. To the right of the dinner plate, place a knife, and to the left, a fork. Place a spoon to the right of the knife.

4. If you have a dessert spoon and/or fork, place them above the plate. The fork's prongs should be facing right, while the spoon bowl (the part that goes in your mouth) should face left.

Table Manners

When you're seated at the table, aim to exercise good table etiquette. You can do so by:[64]

- Placing the napkin on your lap.

- Starting to eat when everyone else does. If you are at a restaurant and you are served your dish first, wait until everyone is served to start eating.

- Sitting up straight.

- Chewing with your mouth closed and not talking when you have food in your mouth.

- Keeping elbows off the table.

---

[64] Emily Post Etiquette, n.d.

- Avoiding burping, passing wind, and slurping.
- Making conversation with others.
- Asking to be excused when your meal is over.
- Thanking whoever prepared the meal.
- Offering to help clear the table.

Four Easy, Yummy Recipes to Try

It's time to put the skills you have learned in this chapter to the test. How about making four delicious recipes that you can make in a few minutes? Remember to have your parents or a trusted adult around to make sure the activity remains safe and fun.

CHEESE OMELET

PREPARATION TIME: 5 MINUTES

Serves: 2

Ingredients:

4 large eggs

3 tablespoons grated cheese

A knob of butter

Salt and pepper to taste

Instructions:

Place a pan on the fire and get it to medium heat. Crack the eggs into a bowl, add salt and pepper, and whisk them until they are fluffy. Place the butter into the pan and wait until it melts. Add the eggs and sprinkle the cheese on top. Wait around two or three minutes , then flip the eggs over and cook for another minute or two.

VEGETARIAN PASTA DISH

PREPARATION TIME: 45 MINUTES

Serves: 4

Ingredients:

4 cups of cherry tomatoes

4 cloves of garlic, smashed

1 (8-ounce) block of feta cheese

½ cup of olive oil

Salt and pepper to taste

½ teaspoon of red pepper flakes

Fresh basil leaves for garnish

A pack of pasta

Instructions:

Preheat your oven to 400°F. Take a rectangular baking dish and place the tomatoes, garlic, and olive oil in it. Place the entire block of feta in the center of the pan. Season with salt, pepper, and red pepper flakes. Bake for around 45 minutes. When the dish is done, the feta will have a nice golden-brown color on top. Boil the pasta as long as the package indicates. Drain it, setting aside ¾ cup of the pasta water. Place the pasta, feta mixture, and reserved water in a bowl and stir until the mixture is uniform.

Garnish the pasta with fresh basil leaves.

CHOCOLATE CHIP BANANA ICE-CREAM CUPS
PREPARATION TIME: 5 MINUTES

(though you will have to wait for a total of around five hours until you can enjoy this treat).

Ingredients:

7 ripe bananas

1.5 teaspoons vanilla extract

1/3 cup chocolate chips

(choose chips that are sweetened with

a healthy sweetener like xylitol or stevia)

Instructions:

Place a piece of parchment paper on a tray. Slice the bananas and

place them on the tray, freezing them for around two hours. Place

the frozen bananas into a blender and blend until smooth. Place

the creamy bananas into a bowl and add the chocolate chips,

gently mixing them in until they are uniformly spread. Place the

gently mixing them in until they are uniformly spread. Place the

"ice cream" into silicone muffin molds and sprinkle the top with

more chocolate chips or hundreds-and-thousands. Freeze them for

around three hours. Remove them and allow them to melt for

abou for about three minutes before tucking into them.

DAIRY-FREE RAW CHOCOLATE RECIPE

PREPARATION TIME: 5 MINUTES.

Serves: 4

Ingredients:

1 cup raw cacao butter, chopped

1 cup raw, unsweetened cacao powder

1 cup honey or maple syrup

1 teaspoon vanilla extract

Toppings such as chopped nuts and/or

dried fruit

Instructions:

Melt the cacao butter in a double boiler. This means a bowl that sits securely on a pot of boiling water. Once the cacao is melted, remove it from the heat and add the cacao powder, honey, and vanilla extract, mixing the mixture with a spoon. Drop spoonfuls of the mixture onto a tray lined with wax paper. While the chocolate is still melted, sprinkle your toppings on your chocolate. Place the tray in the fridge or freezer until it is hard and keep it in the fridge as it may melt if left out.

Now that you are a budding chef, you may be wondering what you would do with all the money you earn when you become world-famous. If so, you will find a host of interesting tips on money and budgeting in Chapter Nine!

CHAPTER NINE
Understanding Money and Budgeting

WEEKLY
BUDGET

School Allowance
Accessories
Clothes
Food

"Money without financial intelligence is money soon gone."

– Robert Kiyosaki

O ne in five teens in the US lacks basic financial literacy.[65] What is financial literacy, and why is it so important?

Financial Literacy

Being financially literate is knowing how to spend and save money. The benefits of being financially smart are plentiful. They include:

1. **A bright future.** When you start following healthy financial practices from the time you are a child or tween, you are more likely to make good financial choices when you are an adult. You can boost your chances of being financially independent.

2. **The ability to distinguish between needs and wants.** From a young age, it is essential to differentiate between needs (things you need to survive like food and electricity) and wants (things that enrich life or make them more fun—like a new iPhone or a trendy pair of sneakers).

3. **Confidence when discussing financial activities like saving and investing.** Concepts like saving and investing money sound very complex, but in fact, many kids across the globe are already "making money from their money"

---

[65] NEFE, n.d.

by investing. There are apps and facilities that enable them to do so under the supervision of their parents. When you are older, the way in which you invest your money can have a major impact on your quality of life. Some people who invest wisely retire early, thus having more time to travel, enjoy their favorite hobbies, and be with the people they love.

4. **Understanding the concept of opportunity cost.** The theory of opportunity cost indicates that when you choose one activity, you give up the opportunity to choose other options. Below is an example of an opportunity cost:[66]

   Dan is a 45-year-old with three kids. He has two potential choices:

   1. Continue working and earning a big salary plus benefits.
   2. Becoming a stay-at-home father.

The opportunity cost of choice #1 is missing out on time with his family.

The opportunity cost of choice #2 is missing out on making money during his most vital working years.

There is no right or wrong choice here. It is up to Dan to decide which is the better opportunity for him. He might choose #2, for instance, because he feels that it aligns more closely with his wishes to build a close family. He may think that money can be made at any time, but time with one's children flies so fast.

---

[66] Quan, 2022.

Below are two more examples of opportunity costs:
Mary is a tween who is studying Chinese. She also loves dancing and wants to sign up for hip-hop classes. The only problem is that her Chinese and dancing classes are at the same time.

She has two potential choices:

1. She can continue to study Chinese.
2. She can ditch Chinese and start studying dancing.

Once again, there is no right or wrong choice. Mary may pick #1 because she has big ambitions, and Chinese may be important in her future career. The cost of this choice is that she will not be able to improve her dancing abilities to the extent she wants to. If she chooses #2, it may turn out well for her because dancing fulfills her so much, that sacrificing her language lessons was worth it for her. Mary has to make her decision based on her values, interests, and goals.

Sydney is a 12-year-old girl who is given the opportunity to mow her neighbor's lawn for a set amount of money every week. She can:

1. Accept the job and do all she can to be on time and mow the lawn well.
2. Refuse the job, so she has more time to read and play online with friends.

If she picks #1, she may lose out on an hour of fun. If she chooses #2, she may take much longer to save for that hoverboard she has been eyeing.

Activity Time:

Take your journal and list the opportunity costs of the following actions:

- Continuing to do a sport you don't like when there is another activity you would like to join.

- Spending your allowance at the mall every weekend when you also have the choice to set a bit aside to save for the new hoodie you've been eyeing.

- Asking your parents to raise your allowance in return for doing extra chores.

- Avoiding going to parties because you feel shy about meeting new people.

Saving Money

I remember that when I was in my tweens, I used to save up for the things I wanted to buy. Usually, I would buy books, clothes, shoes, and board games (which I still love). I'll admit that I didn't start "seriously" saving until I was a little older. I had adopted my cute puppy, Wanda, and one day, while talking to a friend, she told me that her dog, Mochi, needed surgery. She told me the bill was around $1,000. I remember thinking that I didn't have that amount in my savings, and I worried about having to ask my family for so much money if something happened to Wanda. I started working at a café while I was studying, and I was so happy to see my savings grow. I soon had more than I needed for emergencies. I also started making wiser financial choices—for instance, getting pet insurance for Wanda. It cost just a few dollars per month, but it covered expenses such as vaccinations and vet visits, and I started breathing a bit easier. Saving money is important because you never know when you or someone you love might be in a bind. What is more, when you are older and retired, it is nice to know that there is enough money in the bank to cover your needs and wants.

Why Is Saving So Important?

Setting money aside from your allowance or any money you earn from other sources teaches you important financial lessons, including:

- *How to buy things you really need or want, instead of*
- *spending impulsively and regretting it later.*
- *The concept of interest (think of interest as a way to "get richer" from the money you already have).*
- *The value of money. It can take many weeks or months to save for something you want. Especially if you have to work or wait for this money, you can begin to understand the value of money and why it should be spent wisely.*
- *The importance of focusing on your goals. Financial goals require commitment.*

A Fun Savings Game for Younger Tweens

Get your hands on a cute piggy bank or box where you can keep your money. Ask your parents if they will be willing to match your savings dollar for dollar, or by a certain percentage. For instance, you might agree with your parents that for every $100 you save, they will give you 10 percent of this amount (or $10).

Opening a Bank Account

Financial experts suggest that most kids are able to grasp money concepts by the time they are nine.[67] Therefore, this is probably a good age at which to open a savings account. You will need your parent or guardian to set up a so-called "custodial account" (also called a "joint account"). Both of you will have access to the account, and the adult can supervise and/or select limits—for instance, on how much you are allowed to withdraw.[68]

You can open either a checking account (which comes with a debit card) or a savings account. Experts recommend that you wait until you are about 15 to open a checking account because it requires more responsibility. You can use a debit card to pay for items, so it is handy to have. However, you need to take good care of it, since cards can be stolen or lost.

---

[67] First National Bank and Trust Company, n.d.
[68] U.S. Bank, 2020.

Withdrawing Money From an ATM

Although you can go to your bank and withdraw money, it is much faster to use an ATM machine. You simply need to insert your debit card into the machine, enter your PIN (Personal Identification Number, which your bank will provide you with), enter the amount you need, then wait for the machine to give you your cash and a receipt.

There may be restrictions on how much cash you can withdraw from an ATM on a single day. Most banks allow you to withdraw cash from an ATM machine for free, but if you use a machine that is owned by another bank, they may charge you a small fee to do so.

When using an ATM machine, always ensure that you remove your card and keep it in a safe place. Some banks have contactless ATMs, which allow you to use your smartphone to withdraw money instead of your card. You will need to have the bank's app installed on your phone. To use this system, approach the ATM, and open the mobile payment app on your phone. Place your phone close to the contactless ATM reader and enter your PIN code to withdraw your cash. People can use an ATM for more than withdrawing money.

Other options include:

- Depositing money
- Checking your balance
- Paying some types of bills

Creating a Budget

Making a budget is an important way to work out how you want to spend your money. Budgets are indispensable throughout your life, as they ensure that you never overspend and that you set enough money aside for a rainy day. To make your budget, follow these steps:[69]

1. **Calculate your income or allowance.** Some people say that a child's age should equal the dollar amount they earn weekly. For instance, a 10-year-old child would earn $10 a week. Of course, the amount you earn is for your family or guardians to decide.

2. **Identify fixed and variable costs.** Think of "fixed" costs as those which are always the same. You may not have many fixed expenses yet at your age, but your parents may have fixed expenses like rent or a mortgage, a car payment, a cell phone, and subscriptions to services like Netflix.

   "Variable" expenses, on the other hand, are those in which the amounts change. Examples of variable expenses include what your parents pay weekly for groceries, going out for lunch or dinner, clothing, and fuel.

---

[69] Mydoh, 2022.

Even if you don't have any fixed and variable expenses of your own, know that these costs will determine what your budget looks like. It is important to pay all bills and purchases on time because if not, you can have late fees and the total amount you will pay will be higher.

3. **Differentiate between needs and wants.** You may need a new hoverboard if yours has broken down. However, you may want a hoverboard from a luxury brand because it is trendy.

4. **Set up a savings goal using the 50/30/20 rule.**
   This is a classic rule for saving that adults use. It involves dividing your monthly income into three spending categories: 50 percent for needs, 30 percent for wants, and 20 percent for savings or paying off debt. For instance, if your allowance is around $50 per month, 50 percent of this (or $25) can go to your needs, 30 percent (or $15) can go to wants, and 20 percent ($10) can go to your savings.

HANDY INFORMATION

Many adults in the US owe large amounts of debt because they overuse credit cards. These cards differ from debit cards because they allow you to borrow money from the bank to buy something, and then pay the bank back monthly. When you use credit cards, you don't just pay back the amount you borrowed. You also pay "interest." Think of interest as the amount the bank gains by loaning you money. When you are old enough to have a credit card, it is essential to look for banks that offer you low interest. It is also vital to calculate how much you can spend so that you don't end up burdened by debt.

Creating a Spending, Saving, and Giving Jar System

You may find it easier to save money by using separate jars for each category. In addition to creating jars for spending and saving, some kids also have giving jars. This jar is for supporting charities that matter to them. You can make old mason jars pretty by printing out labels and pasting them on.[70]

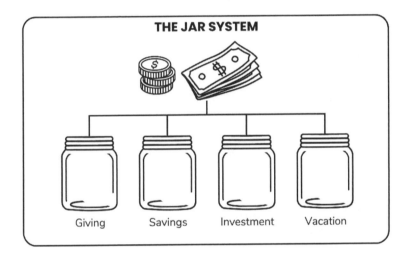

Shopping Wisely

You can lose a lot of money if you simply hit the shops with your wallet in hand and just buy the first cute thing you see. In order to be a smart shopper, take the following steps:

---

[70] Parent Vault, n.d.

Research items before you buy them. Conduct a Google search to check out how much your chosen items are in different physical and online stores. Sometimes, online stores have big sales, and you can buy more than one item for the same price. Researching is also vital because you can read customer reviews of the products you are interested in. An item may look good, but customer reviews may indicate it doesn't last long or looks different in person than in ads.

Buy items at the right time. Brand items often offer big reductions during specific times of the year. Some of the best sales are on Black Friday (which takes place in November), Cyber Monday (the Monday after Black Friday), New Year's Day (when you will find great post-Christmas sales), and the first of September (for post-summer sales).[71]

If you are going to a mall to shop, try to leave home with a set list and stick to it. This will help you stick to your budget.

Keep receipts, so you can return unwanted items if you change your mind when you get home. Most stores won't give you your money back or exchange the unwanted item for a new one if you don't bring them the receipt.

---

[71] Reship, n.d.

Try to think of the environment when you're shopping. Choose companies with sustainable principles and those that package items in eco-friendly materials.

Why Second-Hand Shopping Is Good for the Planet

You can make a big difference to the planet and to people by shopping in second-hand stores and supporting brands that are ethical and environmentally friendly. When you buy second-hand stuff, you can:

1. **Make big savings.** Vintage shops have everything from jeans to jackets and cool accessories. Pay them a visit in case you chance upon a few cool items.

2. **Help save the environment.** Buying pre-loved goods can be considered a type of recycling. Why throw away things that someone else would love to own?

3. **Buy things more frequently while watching your savings grow.** It's nice to feel like you have new things to wear as the seasons change, and you can own more items for a lower price if you shop at second-hand online stores and thrift shops.

What Are Ethical Brands?

Ethical brands are those that treat their employees fairly and do not condone child or forced labor. They make sure their employees are working in comfortable, safe settings. They pay their workers a fair wage and recognize their right to join a union (which protects workers' rights). For instance, ethical fashion brands think about the lifespan of garments. When they design an item, they first think of how to ensure that it is sturdy. They also aim to make products that withstand trends and have a multi-functional quality. Ethical fashion is the opposite of fast fashion, which simply seeks to sell the largest amount in the least amount of time. Fast fashion also exposes workers to abuse, paying them poor wages and unjustly removing many of their rights.

What Are Environmentally Friendly Brands?

Environmentally friendly or sustainable brands aim to reduce the negative impact that their industry has on people, animals, and the planet.[72] They undertake various actions, with many brands relying on renewable energy, recycling materials, minimizing waste, upcycling items, and making sure that they do not pollute waterways with toxic chemicals. They also use less water, use sustainably sourced materials, and pioneer fabrics that will "last a lifetime." Below are just a few examples of what specific brands are achieving:

- **Bureo**, a fashion company in California, works alongside fishing companies in South America. It collects, cleans, and shreds fishing nets and recycles them into a durable material that provides a fair income to local communities.

- **Patagonia** grows its own cotton on dedicated farms. Its aim is to rehabilitate the soil, help local communities, and ensure animal welfare.

---

[72] Mayhead. n.d.

- **Eileen Fisher** takes back items customers no longer use, reselling them, or turning them into new designs. It designs items that are timeless so that they never fall out of fashion. For Days takes back old pieces, giving you a swap credit you can use to buy new clothes. They also make a host of items in eco-friendly materials like organic cotton and recycled terry.

- **Take Sheep Inc.** lets every single person who buys one of their sweaters know the exact sheep it came from. They feed their animals well, allow them to graze freely on pastures, and ensure these furry creatures enjoy a happy, pain-free life.

- **Levi's** is pioneering innovative fabrics like cottonized hemp, which requires fewer resources to produce and is ultra-sturdy.[73]

Now that you are aware of the importance of saving money, making a budget, and shopping wisely, you are probably ready for one of the biggest challenges of all: handling emergencies! You never know when you may need to call the fire brigade, call your parents to pick you up, or need to change a bike tire by yourself. Discover how to do all this in Chapter Ten!

---

[73] Abbas & Shipin, 2022.

CHAPTER TEN
Handling Emergencies

"There's no harm in hoping for the best as long as you're prepared for the worst."

– Stephen King

What would you do if there was a sudden emergency in your home? Would you know who to call and what to say? Although emergencies are rare, it is good to have a "plan of action" in place so that you confidently know the steps to take when you are called upon to save the day.

Important Reading for Tweens and Parents:
A 2021 study by the American Academy of Pediatrics revealed that 91 percent of elementary school kids could not reliably call 911.[74] In the study, the researchers organized a simulation in which an adult began choking and there was a cell phone nearby. In another room, a staff member was ready to receive the call and test the child's ability to communicate the problem. Some of the biggest barriers for kids included:

1. **Locks on cell phones.** Many phones are locked with a password or difficult to navigate, especially if kids don't have the same phone accessible to them in an emergency.

2. **Lack of access to smartphones.** Around 26.6 million kids under the age of 12 have limited or no access to emergency services because they do not have a phone, or they have limited ability and training. Kids living in poverty are more likely to face this issue.[75] If parents wish to give their kids a phone but they are also

[74] Huber et al., 2021.
[75] Cosmo Technologies, 2022.

concerned about screen time, they can buy their tween a phone like Relay, which is screen-free and which allows children to call parents any time they wish.

Dangerous Myths About Kids and Emergencies

Children under the age of 12 are the least disconnected people in the US. Just a few myths that are contributing to the problem include:

1. **Myth One: Children Can't Help**
   Many people underestimate the power of kids to save lives and avoid big disasters by calling emergency services.

2. **Myth Two: Kids Don't Need Emergency Services**
   Children can face a host of emergency situations. They may witness accidents and unintentional injuries, so they may need emergency services more often than people realize.

Crucial Information for Parents

Experts recommend that children begin emergency awareness training at a young age. All children should have access to a phone and learn how to use it in a hands-on way.

Calling 911 in the US (112 if You Are in the UK)

If an emergency happens at home, you should call 911 if you are in the US and 112 if you are in the UK (ask your parents what the right number to remember is if you live in a country that is not the US or UK). Emergencies that require this action include:[76]

- *Fires*
- *Someone who is unconscious*
- *Someone who is having trouble breathing—for instance because they are having an intense asthma flare-up*
- *Someone who is choking*
- *Witnessing a break-in or other criminal activity*
- *A serious car accident*

When the 911 operator answers, they will ask you questions such as:

- *"What is the emergency?" Example answer: "My friend is having an asthma attack and cannot breathe."*

- *"Where are you" or "What is your address?" Example answer: "My name is Tana Freid and we are at #155 Elm Street in El Cerrito."*

- *"Who is with you?" Example answer: "It's just me and my friend."*

- *"Who needs help?" Example answer: "My friend."*

---

[76] KidsHealth, n.d.

TIPS FOR PARENTS

Roleplay 911 calls with your tweens. Make sure they know your home address by heart and leave it written next to the phone so they can provide this information to emergency services if required.

Responding When Someone Is Injured or Seems Unwell: The DRABC Steps

When an injury arises or someone suddenly feels unwell, it is important to carry out an initial assessment or observation of how they are, using five steps that are known by the acronym, DRABC.[77] The five steps are:

1. **Danger.** Look around you and see if there are dangers you need to be aware of before approaching the person. These can include:

   - *Cars on the road*
   - *Broken glass*
   - *A live electrical current*
   - *Fire and/or smoke*

---

[77] Guzder, 2021.

For instance, if there is broken glass near the person and you are barefooted, put your shoes on first. If there is a live electrical current and you know how to do so, switch off the power at the source. If you are unsure how to do this, never touch the person directly. Instead, call 911 immediately.

2. **Response.** Once it is safe to approach the person, talk to them to see if they are responsive. Ask them to look at you, say something, or raise their hand. If they are not responsive, do not shake them because if they have a neck or back injury, this could make it worse. Instead, call 911 and go to the next step.

3. **Airway.** If the person is not responding, tilt their head back gently, lifting their chin. Look to see if there is anything blocking their airway. If there is, carefully remove it. Do not place your fingers in their mouth if you can't see what is there, as this could potentially move something that is blocking their airway further down. Go to the next step.
    If the person is responsive and they are choking, you will need to give them a combination of black slaps and abdominal thrusts.

4. **Breathing.** Check if the person is breathing normally by tilting their head back and looking to see if their chest moves, and you can feel the air from their mouth on your cheek for 10 seconds. If breathing is normal, move to the final step. If not, you will need to perform CPR with rescue breaths. If you are not trained in this method, just give hands-only CPR, without the breaths.

Question Time: What is CPR?

CPR (cardiopulmonary resuscitation) is a way to help a person who has stopped breathing, and whose heart may have stopped beating, stay alive. "Cardio" is centered on the heart and "pulmonary" is all about the lungs.[78] It involves chest compressions (pressing on a person's chest 30 times to move blood through the heart). It also involves giving two rescue breaths to someone after chest compressions if there is nothing in their airway and the person is not breathing.

AN IMPORTANT FACT ON CPR

Experts say that children around 9 years old are ready to learn CPR, but you should receive age-appropriate training. Trained professionals from groups like the American Red Cross, the National Safety Council, or the American Heart Association (in the US) can help you hone your technique and feel more confident about what you are doing. If you are in the UK, contact Little LifeSavers or St. John Ambulance.

5. **Circulation.** If the person is breathing independently, check if they are bleeding anywhere. If they have a wound, apply direct pressure to it with a sterile dressing or clean cloth. You should have called 911 by now. Stay with the person and assure them that help is coming. If the person isn't bleeding but is unresponsive and breathing normally, put them into the recovery position so that their airway is open and they do not choke.

---

[78] Cronan, n.d.

Emergency Awareness...

How to Place Someone in the Recovery Position

1. Place the arm nearest you at a right angle to their body, with their elbow bent and their palm facing the ceiling.

2. Bring the other arm across the chest and place the back of their hand against the cheek that is closest to you. Keep it there. With your other hand, pull the knee that is farthest from you upward until their foot is flat on the floor.

3. Pull on the far left to roll the person toward you. The leg should be bent at a right angle. They will be lying on their side at this stage.

4. Tilt the person's head back gently, lifting their chin to keep their airway open.

5. Call 911 for help.[79]

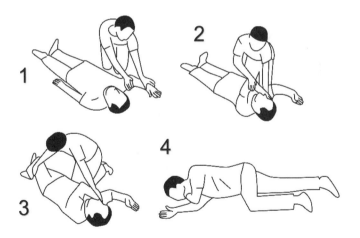

---

[79] St. John Ambulance, n.d.

What to Do After Completing the DRABC Steps?

After completing the above steps, you can work on finding out more about what happened. Observe them and ask them to tell you what happened. Inquire about their symptoms and check their body for any signs of injury or illness. Ask them for important information, using the AMPLE acronym.

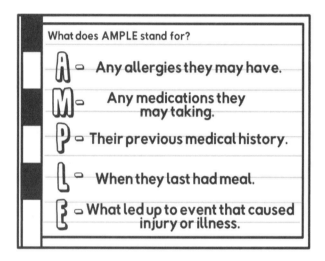

What does AMPLE stand for?

A ▫ Any allergies they may have.

M ▫ Any medications they may taking.

P ▫ Their previous medical history.

L ▫ When they last had meal.

E ▫ What led up to event that caused injury or illness.

First Aid Tips

You can learn many more important pieces of information by joining the Scouts or taking a first aid course. By the time you are in your late tweens, you should know the following measures:

- Apply pressure to a bleeding wound
- Put ice on a swollen injury (like a sprain)

- Apply cold running water to a burn
- Pinch the nostrils for around 10 minutes for a nosebleed
- Place a blanket over someone in shock
- Gently roll someone over into the recovery position as indicated above

Now that you are up to speed with emergency care, you may be ready to move on to the final chapter on how to take care of your bike, electric scooter, and hoverboard!

Take some time to learn FIRST AID and CPR. It saves lives and it works.

CHAPTER ELEVEN
Maintaining Your Bike, Electric Scooter, and Hoverboard

"Nothing compares to the simple pleasure of a bike ride."

– John F. Kennedy

O ne of the best things about being a tween is riding your bike, electric scooter, or hoverboard. In this chapter, learn how to keep them in good condition so they stand the test of time!

Ensuring Your Bike Is in Good Condition

Your bike can be a handy vehicle to have around when you are a tween. It can get you to places quickly, cheaply, and sustainably. Make sure it is in great shape for years by paying attention to the following:[80]

- **Air:** Make sure your tires have the pressure recommended by the manufacturer. You can check the pressure by placing a gauge on the valve and pressing it downward until the needle on the gauge moves and shows the pressure amount. You may need to ask a parent to help you out with this task the first time. If pressure is lacking, you can easily inflate it with a pump. The pump shows you the pressure amount, and you can keep adding air until you reach the correct level.

- **Brakes:** Before leaving home, apply pressure to your front and back brakes. If they are not working, ask your parent to help or take the bike to a professional to have them fixed.

---

[80] Woom, n.d.

- **Chain:** Clean and oil your chain frequently so that it does not become rusty or lodged with dirt.
- **Performing the Drop Test:** Before leaving home, lift your bike by the seat about six inches off the ground and drop it. Listen for any rattling or loose parts and let your parent know if anything sounds odd.

How to Change a Bike Tire

If your tire goes flat and you need to change it, know that you can learn to do so quickly and effectively in no time! Follow these steps:

1. Remove the tire and tube, prying under the bead of the tire and hooking it to a spoke and inserting another lever. Slide the second lever under the rim to release the tire.

2. Remove the damaged tube and turn the tire inside-out, looking for any items that may be lodged there. Use gloves, as there may be glass or other sharp objects in the tire that can hurt you.

3. Inflate the new or patched tube slightly (not fully) and insert the valve stem into the hole in the rim.

4. Fit the tube completely into the tire.

5. Check to see if the tube is well-placed and make sure that it isn't pinched between the tire and the rim.

6. Now you can fully inflate the tire. The bead should be seated well into the rim of the tire. If it's not, let a little air out and position the bead well in

the rim. Reinstall the wheel and make sure it rotates well and is properly centered between the brakes.

Taking Care of Your Electric Scooter

If you have an electric scooter, you can boost its functionality and extend its life by:[81]

1. Cleaning it regularly. Give it a good wipe with a cloth that has been dipped in warm water and dish soap. Drain the cloth and wash components like the brakes, handlebars, and lights.

2. Wash the wheels. This time, use a wet rag to remove grime but do not use soap.

3. Degrease the chain. Use water, eco-wash, and a brush to gently scrub your chain. Use water to remove excess dirt. Dry the chain completely, then add a small amount of lubricant that is specifically made for electric scooters.

4. Check your tires to make sure they have the right pressure.

5. Recharge your battery, aiming not to let it go below 50 percent capacity. This will extend the life of your battery.

6. Have your brakes serviced as recommended by the manufacturer.

---

[81] Hayes, 2021.

Taking Care of Your Hoverboard

Hoverboards are another fun way to get from point A to B quickly and effortlessly. To ensure your hoverboard stands the test of time:[82]

1. Clear your hoverboard and its wheels with a wet rag, removing grime and dust.

2. Ensure your battery is always well-charged.

3. Give your hoverboard time to cool completely if you have been using it for an extended amount of time.

4. Check the stability of the paddles. They should feel stable, and they should not be loose. Paddles can actually loosen and detach at any time, so get help from a professional if they don't feel as tight as usual.

With all maintenance and cleaning chores, it's a good idea to practice a few times first with an adult or professional who knows the ins and outs of maintaining your vehicles and devices and keeping them safe.

SAFETY TIP!

To avoid accidents, keep away from main or busy roads when you are using a hoverboard.

---

[82] Hoverboards NZ, n.d.

Safety Outside the Home

Safety also involves watching out for potential dangers when you are walking home from school, walking to a friend's house, or visiting a public place such as a mall. To ensure you are safe when you are outside the home:

- Keep a charged cell phone with you at all times when you are away from home.

- Make sure your parents can track you if necessary via the GPS system in your cell phone.

- Trust your instincts.

- Avoid being out alone in the late afternoon or evening.

- Install a child phone tracking app on your phone, so your parents always know where you are.

As you can see, safety involves almost all aspects of your life—from the way you interact with others online, to taking care of your bike, scooter, or hoverboard!

Conclusion

"There is always one moment in childhood when the door opens and lets the future in."

– Graham Greene

T he tween years are a unique time in life in which you can still enjoy being a kid, but also look forward to the independence that comes with one's teen years. Once you reach the age of 13 or 14, life may seem to be going too quickly to keep up with it, as you start preparing for young adulthood, college, and/or your professional life.

The skills you learn when you are young—everything from how to make an omelet to how to change a bike tire—will stand you in good stead for the rest of your life. Think of how cool it would be to surprise your parents with breakfast in bed, have a super-organized room, or enter an exam with the confidence that arises when you know you're simply there to share the knowledge you already possess.

As you read through this book, you may find that some skills are easier to master than others. For instance, it may take one or two goes to make the perfect raw chocolate treat, but it may take longer than this to learn how to read others' body language or to resolve conflicts with a "win-win" mentality. My aim isn't to try to turn you into a perfect, "robotic" person, but rather, to provide you with tips for different areas of life you may wish to improve.

If you are reading this Conclusion, it means that you have made it through an array of topics—including how to make friends, be confident, make good decisions, solve problems, and be resilient. You also found practical advice on everyday aspects such as keeping your room tidy, cooking and tidying up, and handling emergencies confidently.

Mastering all the strategies and methods will take commitment, courage, and self-kindness. Remember to keep a journal, so you can observe which strategies work best for you, and which need

refinement. If one strategy doesn't work, don't immediately rule it out. Try it out a few times; it may work better the second time around.

As you are trying out the different tips and techniques I have shared, embrace the growth mentality. Remember that nobody is born with a fixed number of talents and abilities. Each and every one of us can learn, improve, and grow. In moments in which you find that you are doubting yourself, rely on practices such as journaling, mindfulness meditation, and reframing negative thoughts into positive ones by looking at the available evidence.

Finally, don't forget to have fun with all the skills you learn in this book. If your pasta is overdone, your chocolate lacks sugar, or your hands get dirty while cleaning your hoverboard, remember that these wonderful "disasters" are part of the learning process. Never lose your sense of curiosity, amazement, and wonder. These qualities mark childhood, but if you play your cards right, you can carry them with you for the rest of your days.

Finally, I have a small favor to ask. If you found this book helpful, I would love it if you could leave me a review on Amazon. My aim is to support tweens by helping them hone the skills they need to shine in social and practical settings. If the methods I shared helped you, enable me to reach more people who may need help through your words. Thank you for reading!

THANKS FOR READING MY BOOK!

I sincerely hope you enjoyed this book, and that you will benefit from implementing the Skills discussed.

I would be incredibly grateful if you could take a few seconds to leave me an honest review or a star-rating on Amazon. (A star-rating only takes a couple of clicks).

Your review helps other young adults discover this book, and may also help them on their life journey. It will also be good Karma for you.

Scan this code to leave a review.

SOMETHING FOR YOU!

Get your printable workbook today!

Scan this code to download.

IF YOU FIND THIS BOOK HELPFUL, YOU MIGHT ALSO LOVE:

Here's what others are saying about Vivian:

 Sunshine87

★★★★★ **Love it!**
Reviewed in the United States us on January 26, 2023
Verified Purchase

I've read several of Foster's book and not one of them has been a disappointment!! I loved the fun facts, the not so fun facts, the FAQ, and the true stories sprinkled through this book! Truly a great resource for any teen or anyone for that matter!

 "randfilms"

★★★★★ **Such an important and valuable book for today's kids**
Reviewed in the United States us on January 13, 2023
Verified Purchase

Okay, so I did jump the gun reading this. My kid is not even 5 yet. But I found this book a great source of information and actionable items, especially based on how I see teen kids behaving today. There's so much pressure on kids that I wanted to get ahead of the game and this book served as a sort of North Star for knowledge I can implement as my son gets older. Well done. Recommend.

 Guznag

★★★★★ **Grow in life**
Reviewed in the United States us on January 7, 2023
Verified Purchase

Teenagers should read this book to learn about the life skills they will need. Focus is placed on a variety of topics, including how to keep your house clean, how to take care of your physical and mental health, and how to save money. The emphasis on attending classes and how to decide whether or not to take out student loans is something I really appreciate. The information about setting up appropriate boundaries is also something I really like. This book contains a wealth of knowledge on a variety of skills and subjects that are frequently not taught in schools yet are crucial to have.

 Scan this code to check-out Vivian's other books.

References

Abbas, T., & Shipin, S. (2022, April 22). *31 sustainable fashion brands you can shop confidently.* Glamour. https://www.glamour.com/story/sustainable-fashion-brands

A. C. (2022, September 10). *10+ goal setting statistics you should know (facts and studies).* HQ Hire. https://hqhire.com/goal-setting-statistics/

Blue Flame Kitchen. (n.d.). *How to safely handle a knife.* https://www.atcoblueflamekitchen.com/en-ca/how-to/knife-safety-kids.html

Boogaard, K. (2021, December 26). *How to write SMART goals.* Atlassian. https://www.atlassian.com/blog/productivity/how-to-write-smart-goals#:~:text=The%20SMART%20in%20SMART%20goals,within%20a%20certain%20time%20frame

Brown-Riggs, C. (2017, September 6). *New research finds parents lack confidence to cook.* HuffPost. https://www.huffpost.com/entry/new-research-finds-parent_b_11874326

Brownstein, J., & Chitale, R. (2008, September 17). *10 germy surfaces you touch every day.* ABC News. https://abcnews.go.com/Health/ColdandFluNews/story?id=5727571&page=1

Brunier, G., Graydon, J., Rothman, B., Sherman C., & Liadsky, R. (2002, March 13). The psychological well-being of renal peer support volunteers. *Journal of Advanced Nursing, 38*(1), 40–49. https://doi.org/10.1046/j.1365-2648.2002.02144.x

But First Joy. (n.d.). *10 positive affirmations for teens and young adults (Free printables)*. https://butfirstjoy.com/positive-affirmations-for-teens-young-adults/

Calm Kids. (2022, February 10). *Why do children need to be mindful?* https://www.calm-kids.com/blog/why-do-children-need-to-be-mindful

Cario, J. (2022, August 6). *How to help children stop comparing themselves to others.* Big Life Journal. https://biglifejournal.com/blogs/blog/how-to-help-children-stop-comparing-themselves-to-others

Centers for Disease Control and Prevention. (n.d.-a). *Data and statistics on children's mental health.* https://www.cdc.gov/childrensmentalhealth/data.html

Centers for Disease Control and Prevention. (n.d.-b). *Prevalence of childhood obesity in the United States.* https://www.cdc.gov/obesity/data/childhood.html

Centers for Disease Control and Prevention. (n.d.-c). *Progress on children eating more fruit, not vegetables.* https://www.cdc.gov/vitalsigns/fruit-vegetables/infographic.html

Chalmers, A. (2022, October 17). *Does using a dishwasher actually save water?* The Spruce. https://www.thespruce.com/does-using-a-dishwasher-actually-save-water-5218699#:~:text=The%20Short%20Answer%3A%20Yes,water%20weekly%2C%E2%80%9D%20Klien%20adds

Choc. (n.d.). *The rewards of giving back.* https://www.choc.org/health-topics/rewards-of-giving-back/#:~:text=Community%20service%20can%20show%20kids,person%20can%20make%20a%20difference

Choose FI Foundation. (n.d.). *10 scary financial literacy statistics.* https://www.choosefifoundation.org/blog/scary%20financial%20literacy%20statistics

Collins, L. M. (2022, September 12). *How cleaning helps young adults launch.* Deseret News. https://www.deseret.com/2022/9/11/23329232/how-cleaning-helps-young-adults-launch-college-roommates

Cosmo Technologies. (2022). *Kids disconnected: Examining children's dangerous lack of access to 9-1-1 emergency services.* https://cdn.shopify.com/s/files/1/0420/6949/1880/files/COSMO_9 11_Calling_Report__FINALv2.pdf?v=1659014805

Cronan, K. (n.d.). *CPR: A real lifesaver.* KidsHealth. https://kidshealth.org/en/kids/cpr.html#:~:text=CPR%20(cardiopul monary%20resuscitation)%20is%20a,Resuscitation%22%20mean s%20%22revive.%22

Dellner, A. (2022, July 29). *The pandemic taught us that kids are resilient. Parents are not.* PureWow. https://www.purewow.com/family/pandemic-resilience-kids-parents

Egelnick, M. (2018, August 30). *Tesla CEO Elon Musk reminds us about the importance of delegating work.* KRP. https://www.krp.ca/tesla-ceo-elon-musk-reminds-us-about-the-importance-of-delegating-work

Emily Post Etiquette. (n.d.). *Download: Top table manners for kids.* https://emilypost.com/advice/top-table-manners-for-kids

Encourage Play. (n.d.). *21 places to make new friends—A list of social activities for kids.* https://www.encourageplay.com/blog/6-places-to-make-connections

https://www.health.harvard.edu/healthbeat/learning-diaphragmatic-breathing

Hayes, N. (2021, September 24). *Scooter guide.* https://scooter.guide/crucial-tips-for-maintaining-your-electric-scooter/

Hoverboards NZ. (n.d.). *Five effective maintenance tips for your hoverboard.* https://hoverboardnz.co.nz/blog/five-effective-maintenance-tips-for-your-hoverboard/

Huber, J. F., Davis, S., Phan, J., Jegathesan, T., Campbell, D. D., Chau, R., & Walsh, C. M. (2021, April 1). Children's ability to call 911 in an emergency: A simulation study. *Pediatrics, 147*(4). https://doi.org/10.1542/peds.2020-010520

Jay. (2022, March 18). *10 famous people with a growth mindset.* Mind by Design. https://www.mindbydesign.io/famous-people-with-a-growth-mindset/

Kiddy Charts. (n.d.). *Mindful mantras for kids free printables.* https://www.kiddycharts.com/printables/mindful-mantras-for-kids/

KidsHealth. (n.d.). *Teaching your child how to use 911.* https://kidshealth.org/en/parents/911.html#:~:text=Kids%20should%20make%20sure%20they,address%20and%20phone%20number%20memorized

Kirschner, H., Kuyken, W., Wright, K., Roberts, H., Brejcha, C., & Karl, A. (2019, February 6). Soothing your heart and feeling connected: A new experimental paradigm to study the benefits of self-compassion. *Clinical Psychological Science, 7*(3), 545–565. https://doi.org/10.1177/2167702618812438

LaMagna, M. (2016, September 10). *Why millennials don't know how to cook.* MarketWatch.

https://www.marketwatch.com/story/why-millennials-dont-know-how-to-cook-2016-08-10

Louick, R. (2022a, June 25). *Growth mindset vs. fixed mindset: Key differences and how to shift your child's mindset.* Big Life Journal. https://biglifejournal.com/blogs/blog/growth-mindset-vs-fixed-mindset-differences-and-how-to-shift-your-childs-mindset

Louick, R. (2022b, October 3). *7 ways to teach kids failure is a great thing.* Big Life Journal. https://biglifejournal.com/blogs/blog/help-kids-overcome-fear-failure

MacIntosh, B. R., Murias, J. M., Keir, D. A., & Weir, J. M. (2021, September). What is moderate to vigorous exercise intensity? *Frontiers in Physiology, 22.* https://doi.org/10.3389/fphys.2021.682233

Make Me Better. (2022, September 30). *Identify your strengths.* https://www.makemebetter.net/importance-of-identifying-your-strengths-and-weaknesses/

Mathers, C. (2020, December 1). *10 SMART goals examples for kids.* Develop Good Habits. https://www.developgoodhabits.com/smart-goals-kids/

Mayhead, J. (n.d.). *Every question you've ever had about ethical fashion, answered.* Ethical Made Easy. https://ethicalmadeeasy.com/what-is-ethical-fashion/

Mayo Clinic. (n.d.-a). *Mediterranean diet for heart health.* https://www.mayoclinic.org/healthy-lifestyle/nutrition-and-healthy-eating/in-depth/mediterranean-diet/art-20047801

Mayo Clinic. (n.d.-b). *Teens and social media use: What's the impact?* https://www.mayoclinic.org/healthy-lifestyle/tween-and-teen-health/in-depth/teens-and-social-media-use/art-

20474437#:~:text=Social%20media%20harms,people's%20lives
%20and%20peer%20pressure

Medline Plus. (n.d.). *Facts about saturated fats.*
https://medlineplus.gov/ency/patientinstructions/000838.htm

Meredith, G. R., Rakow, D. A., Eldermire, E. R. B., Madsen, C. G.,
Shelley, S. P., & Sachs, N. A. (2020, January 14). Minimum time
dose in nature to positively impact the mental health of college-
aged students, and how to measure it: A scoping review.
Frontiers in Psychology, 10.
https://doi.org/10.3389/fpsyg.2019.02942

Money Prodigy. (n.d.). *26 goals for teenagers (teenage goal setting
help).* https://www.moneyprodigy.com/goals-for-teenagers/

Morin, A. (n.d.). *4 parts of a conversation: How to help kids with
social skills issues navigate.* Understood.
https://www.understood.org/en/articles/4-parts-of-a-
conversation-how-to-help-kids-with-social-skills-issues-navigate

Mydoh. (2022, September 19). *How to create a budget for kids &
teens.* https://www.mydoh.ca/learn/money-101/money-
basics/how-to-create-a-budget-for-kids-and-teens/

NEFE. (n.d.). *Can America compete? 1 in 5 U.S. teens lacks basic
personal finance skills.* https://www.nefe.org/news/nefe-
digest/2017/can-america-
compete.aspx#:~:text=Results%20from%20the%20Program%20f
or,followed%20by%20Belgium%20and%20Canada

The Nourished Child. (2021, June 11.). *The Mediterranean diet (for
kids).* https://thenourishedchild.com/mediterranean-diet-for-kids/

Oberle, E., Ji, X. R., Kerai, S., Guhn, M., Schonert-Reichl, K. A., &
Gadermann, A. M. (2020, December). Screen time and

extracurricular activities as risk and protective factors for mental health in adolescence: A population-level study. *Preventive Medicine, 141.* https://doi.org/10.1016/j.ypmed.2020.106291

Osmo. (2020, October 7). *8 indoor fun games to improve your child's decision-making skills.* https://blog.playosmo.com/8-indoor-fun-games-to-improve-your-childs-decision-making-skills/

PACER. (n.d.). *Bullying statistics: By the numbers.* https://www.pacer.org/bullying/info/stats.asp

Parent Vault. (n.d.). *How to make a budget: DIY spend, save, give jars (free printable labels).* https://parentvault.com/how-to-make-a-budget-diy-spend-save-give-jars-free-printable-labels/

Pot, J. (2022, October 19). *The 8 best apps to help you focus and block distractions in 2023.* Zapier. https://zapier.com/blog/stay-focused-avoid-distractions/

Prescilla, A. (2020, November 25). *5 benefits of goal setting for children.* LinkedIn. https://www.linkedin.com/pulse/5-benefits-goal-setting-children-amali-prescilla/

Quan, M. (2022, April 25). *How to use opportunity cost to make a better decision.* Financially Alert. https://www.financiallyalert.com/how-to-use-opportunity-cost-to-make-a-better-decision/

Raddish Kids. (n.d.). *Kitchen glossary.* https://www.raddishkids.com/blogs/bonus-bites/kitchen-glossary

Raising Children. (n.d.-a). *Active listening with pre-teens and teenagers.* https://raisingchildren.net.au/pre-teens/communicating-relationships/communicating/active-listening

Raising Children. (n.d.-b). *Muscle relaxation activity for children, teenagers, and parents.* https://raisingchildren.net.au/guides/activity-guides/wellbeing/muscle-relaxation-activity-children-parents

Recker, J. (2019, February 5). *Scientists find a possible link between gut bacteria and depression.* Smithsonian Magazine. https://www.smithsonianmag.com/science-nature/scientists-find-possible-link-between-gut-bacteria-and-depression-180971411/

Renaissance. (n.d.). *What is growth mindset?* https://www.renaissance.com/edword/growth-mindset/#:~:text=without%20effort.%E2%80%9D%20(-,Dweck%2C%202015),Dweck%2C%202015)

Renner, B. (2018, March 21). *American families spend just 37 minutes of quality time together per day, survey finds.* Study Finds. https://studyfinds.org/american-families-spend-37-minutes-quality-time/#:~:text=A%20new%20survey%20found%20that,common%20activity%20is%20significantly%20low

Reship. (n.d.). *America's biggest sale days of the year.* https://blog.reship.com/americas-biggest-sale-days-of-the-year/

Response Institute. (n.d.). *What age should children learn CPR?* https://www.cprconsultants.com/what-age-should-children-learn-cpr/

Rutter, M. (2003, October). Developmental catch-up, and deficit, following adoption after severe global early privation. *Journal of Child Psychology and Psychiatry, 39*(4), 465–476. https://doi.org/10.1111/1469-7610.00343

Scholastic. (n.d.). *5 Internet safety tips for tweens & teens.* https://www.scholastic.com/parents/family-life/social-emotional-learning/technology-and-kids/5-internet-safety-tips-tweens-and-teens.html

Sileo, F. (2018, April 3). *What is meditation? A guide for parents of children and teens.* American Psychological Association. https://www.maginationpressfamily.org/mindfulness-kids-teens/what-is-meditation/#:~:text=Types%20of%20Meditation%20for%20Children,with%20his%20body%20and%20mind

Sleep Foundation. (2022, March 11). *How to determine poor sleep quality.* https://www.sleepfoundation.org/sleep-hygiene/how-to-determine-poor-quality-sleep

Speech and Language Kids. (n.d.). *Teach perspective-taking to children.* https://www.speechandlanguagekids.com/how-to-teach-perspective-talking-to-children/

Spruce, H. (2016, February 26). *10 kitchen safety rules that children need to know.* High Speed Training. https://www.highspeedtraining.co.uk/hub/children-kitchen-safety-rules/

St. John Ambulance. (n.d.). *How to put an adult in the recovery position.* https://www.sja.org.uk/get-advice/first-aid-advice/unresponsive-casualty/how-to-do-the-recovery-position/

Tufts. (2019, September 17). *28% of Americans can't cook.* https://www.nutritionletter.tufts.edu/general-nutrition/28-of-americans-cant-cook/

Uccelli, M. M., Mohr, L. M., & Mohr, D. C. (2004, February). Peer support groups in multiple sclerosis: Current effectiveness and future directions. *Multiple Sclerosis Journal, 10*(1), 16–25. https://doi.org/10.1191/1352458504ms973oa

The University of Queensland. (n.d.). *Self-esteem and self-confidence.* https://my.uq.edu.au/information-and-services/student-support/health-and-wellbeing/self-help-resources/self-esteem-and-self-confidence

University of Rochester Medical Center. (n.d.). *Understanding the teen brain.* https://www.urmc.rochester.edu/encyclopedia/content.aspx?ContentTypeID=1&ContentID=3051

The University of Texas Permian Basin. (n.d.). *How much of communication is nonverbal?* https://online.utpb.edu/about-us/articles/communication/how-much-of-communication-is-nonverbal/

U.S. Bank. (2020, August 5). *5 tips for parents opening a bank account for kids.* https://www.usbank.com/financialiq/manage-your-household/personal-finance/tips-for-parents-opening-bank-account-for-kids.html

ViewSonic. (2022, October 24). *Do you know the best positioning for your computer screen?* https://www.viewsonic.com/library/business/best-computer-screen-positioning/

Watts, A. (n.d.). *7 confidence-building activities for kids.* iMom. https://www.imom.com/7-confidence-building-activities-kids/

Werner, E. E., & Smith, R. S. (2001). *Journeys from childhood to midlife.* Ithaca, NY: Cornell University Press.

What To Get My. (n.d.). *Why it is important to look at things from a different perspective: 5 vital reasons.* https://whattogetmy.com/why-is-it-important-to-look-at-things-from-a-different-perspective/

Wong, K. (2021, May 6). *18 fixed mindset vs growth mindset examples.* The Millennial Grid. https://millennial-grind.com/18-fixed-mindset-vs-growth-mindset-examples/

Woom. (n.d.). *A kids bike safety checklist.* https://woom.com/en_US/check-your-woom-bike-it-s-as-easy-as-abcd

Work for Your Beer. (n.d.). *Sit at a desk all day? The "90-90-90" position that could save you from back, neck, arm & hand pain.* https://workforyourbeer.com/blog/sit-at-a-desk-all-day-the-90-90-90-position-that-could-save-you-from-back-neck-arm-hand-pain/

Zabell, S. (n.d.). *Parenting tweens: How to handle a tween's need for privacy.* Your Teen. https://yourteenmag.com/teenager-school/teenager-middle-school/tweens-need-privacy

Zolkoski, S. M., & Bullock, L. M. (2012, September 5). Resilience in children and youth: A review. *Children and Youth Services Review, 34*, 2295–2303. http://dx.doi.org/10.1016/j.childyouth.2012.08.009

Zom, A. M. (2020, March 5). *Ironing tasks kids can do.* Bounce Back Parenting. https://bouncebackparenting.com/ironing-tasks-kids-can-do/#:~:text=With%20some%20supervision%20and%20training,the%20soleplate%20and%20getting%20burned